ON

GREAT MINDS

Your World...Your Future...YOUR WORDS

- Inspirations From South & South East England Vol II

Edited by Donna Samworth

YoungWriters
First published in Great Britain in 2005 by:
Young Writers
Remus House
Coltsfoot Drive
Peterborough
PE2 9JX
Telephone: 01733 890066
Website: www.youngwriters.co.uk

SB ISBN 1 84602 212 6

Foreword

This year, the Young Writers' 'Great Minds' competition proudly presents a showcase of the best poetic talent selected from over 40,000 up-and-coming writers nationwide.

Young Writers was established in 1991 to promote the reading and writing of poetry within schools and to the youth of today. Our books nurture and inspire confidence in the ability of young writers and provide a snapshot of poems written in schools and at home by budding poets of the future.

The thought, effort, imagination and hard work put into each poem impressed us all and the task of selecting poems was a difficult but nevertheless enjoyable experience.

We hope you are as pleased as we are with the final selection and that you and your family continue to be entertained with *Great Minds - Inspirations From South & South East England Vol II* for many years to come.

Contents

Archbishop Tenison's CE High School, Croydon

The Poems

Sonnet

Walking over the ground covered in leaves
A dull, dark night with a misty full moon
Seeing a girl lying under the tree
I noticed she had been killed by a loon
When I saw her dead I shivered with fright
Her body lay naked under the sky
I heard werewolves screaming in the dark night
Her ghostly eyes looked up to ask me why
Although she was dead I could see her tears
Her face was as dull as the misty fog
Her clothes looked like she'd lived in them for years
Her soul had floated away in the smog
I now know of the real reason for death
So sad she did not live another breath.

Andres Charles (12)
Abbey Wood School, Abbey Wood

Sonnet

After a very peaceful life comes death;
All of your family cannot believe
That you have finally been laid to rest,
Then all of your family start to grieve.
Some of your family will be selfish
They will want all of your precious money.
Spend it on very expensive shellfish
Thinking to themselves, *it's really funny.*
Some won't be able to get over it
Whilst others will think their world has ended,
Others will just stare into space and sit
At least there's memories that are splendid.
Sometimes people will come and see your grave,
Sometimes other people are not as brave.

Danny Locke (13)
Abbey Wood School, Abbey Wood

Football

You roll as quick as a flash of lightning
Spi`nning and bouncing all over the ground
Going into the crowd must be frightening
Hearing the screaming must be a loud sound
Helping your team score in the match to win
Playing in those different divisions
Challenging players get hit in the chin
Never making none of the decisions
With the photographs making a flash
Not yet won but still shining in the sun
Going into the wall with a big bash
Your team has scored a hat-trick, you have won
Following the rules of the FA
But the game's finished, you don't have to play.

Sorcha Crowley (12)
Abbey Wood School, Abbey Wood

Why Hate When We Can Love?

I wonder why life is so miserable
Maybe it's because of all the hate and animosity,
Violence all around, it's almost unbelievable.
Why are people so repulsive and full of eccentricity?

I guess I don't belong here.
There's probably another world for me,
Where ferocity you never hear.
Everyone is kind and loads of things are free.

Brothers, what don't you understand?
Is it the part about relationships
Or the fact that we need each other's hand?
We all need each other, especially strong friendships.

The world would be a better place
If we all loved and never showed disgrace!

Joanitan Nakaweesa (13)
Abbey Wood School, Abbey Wood

Love

You whisper into my ear as soft as summer breeze,
Please don't leave because I was a fool who didn't have
strength to walk away,
Any time I think about you I freeze,
Because you make me want to call it a day.

The day turns into night as I sit down, crossing my legs,
Yet I still keep on thinking about you,
Your lips taste like roses that are red,
My African queen, I wish I never met you with your mannerless boobs.

Love is a game that I played and lost, should have learnt my lesson,
1 kiss, 2 kiss, you were all on my neck then,
When I remember the first day it brings me blessing,
You used to wake me up like a jumping hen.

I just feel like going out on a date again,
But I bet you think I'm insane.

Toby Amusan (13)
Abbey Wood School, Abbey Wood

The Night Killer

As I watch the children die,
The blood in my heart pumps.
I killed them all before they had lunch.
I just think, *why oh why, I lie*
This, friend, I will never do again.
I will not let people die.
If I do this it will make my mum cry.
For I will never do this again for inside me there no longer exists.
This is a killing spree that I do to thee,
Is an expression of my childhood.
I have not killed more than the fare three.
Today is my day to be good.
The Pope is the man that inspired me.
Today I am in an intolerable mood.

Abilio Joao (13)
Abbey Wood School, Abbey Wood

Happiness

Another beautiful day as I open the blind
Flowers are growing and birds singing
As I sit here thinking about something in my mind
I go downstairs and hear the phone ringing
I smell the coffee, deliciously waiting
Quickly need to get dressed
I ask my sister, 'What are you doing?'. Reply: 'I'm tracing.'
Then my mum comes down looking depressed
I step outside to collect the newspaper
The sun shining, children playing
I quickly get my shoes on and shout out, 'See you later.'
I go to the mosque and start praying
I look up in the sky like I am amazed
Then think to myself, *one day I will be praised.*

Abshir Ahmed (13)
Abbey Wood School, Abbey Wood

Frightened . . .

Running and running, I lose my breath,
Scared he might see me,
I can hear his footsteps, I'm scared to death,
I'm hiding in the forest, has he found me?
He's coming closer, I'm starting to sweat,
I want to run but can't,
It started when I was in the pub, that's where we met,
He wants to kill me, should I fight? No, I shan't.
I think he's seen me, he's seen my eye,
Do you think I'm in trouble?
Should I tell the truth or should I lie?
There's something on my hand, it's rubble,
He's found me, I look at him, I think he's mad,
But oh, it's just my sweet, loving dad.

Shanice Sawopa (12)
Abbey Wood School, Abbey Wood

Perish Is My Wish

Take the fun out of living,
Stop love gradually spreading.
Give hatred and pain to all who care,
Ruin everyone, don't leave a spare.

Slam happiness in children's faces,
Hurry up their foot paces.
For death to come amongst them,
When will my love come, when?

Was I a selfish human in life,
For you to grab hold of my wife?
The only person who ever dared
To decrease her life, just from one stare.

Neither value, nor good is left in my life,
No reason for me not to join my wife.

Dilek Ozsahin (13)
Abbey Wood School, Abbey Wood

My Garden

My garden is full of different sounds,
Birds start to sing and the sun starts to shine.
There is always fresh grass on the ground,
That has rich soil and is simply fine.

When I stand in my garden, everything blooms,
I'm surrounded by flowers around my feet.
It's so magical, it's like my bedroom,
That when I'm there it's like a pleasant treat.

When I hear the soft wind I feel so free,
I feel like I've had a golden potion.
When I feel the breeze it's like a sweet dream,
When it rains it's like the deep blue ocean.

As I leave it's like the whole place hardens,
There's no place like my magical garden.

Priya Gangotra (13)
Abbey Wood School, Abbey Wood

The Admirer

It's you I admire
You are my desire
I want to see you smile
As we walk down that aisle
The look in your eyes
As our new baby cries
Your face is so fine
I hope you'll always be mine
As our baby grows
Our love continually flows
You're covered with beauty
And you're such a cutie
I hope we can stay together
As my love for you flows forever.

Jordan Fisher (13)
Abbey Wood School, Abbey Wood

The Meaning Of Love

What is the meaning of love?
Loving someone with all your heart
Our souls together, never being apart
Although my heart is far away
I'll always be by your side
Forever and ever my heart and soul will stay
Stay with you forever, my love will never hide
No one can take you away from me
You're my sweetness and light
You're my eyes to let me see
I just want to hold you forever day and night
My love for you is always there
Because I know this love is in a good care.

Nhung Vu (12)
Abbey Wood School, Abbey Wood

How Do I Love You?

(Inspired by 'How Do I Love Thee? Let Me Count The Ways' by Elizabeth Barrett Browning)

How do I love you? Let me count the ways
I love you like an astronomer loves the stars
And times when you're not with me I wonder where you are
I love you 'cause you know just what to say
What to say to come and take my breath away
I'm serious about us, on you I've set my heart
Say you're serious too, and let nothing set us apart
How do I love you? I haven't finished counting the ways
How do I love you?

I love you like God loves a child
Like a newborn loves breast milk
Hyenas love the wild
It's a blessing you're there when good times aren't
Describe you with beautiful colours is something I can't.

Grace Olaniyi (13)
Abbey Wood School, Abbey Wood

The Blue-Eyed Boy

Look at those deep blue eyes
Eyes that melt my heart
My body shivers like a leaf stuck on a tree
When I look at your deep blue eyes

Those eyes so bright they sparkle in the sun
When you blink it's like Heaven
Heaven only experienced on Earth
Heaven is what I see
When I look in your eyes

When am I going to see Heaven again?
When am I going to see those eyes again?
See that twinkle in your eye
Experience Heaven again
When I look in your eyes.

Ruvimbo Chinzou (13)
Abbey Wood School, Abbey Wood

Never-Ending Love

How do I love you? For my family these are the ways.
I love you with all my heart.
To the end as from the start.
You are with me every day and every night.
I love you forever and always.
You help me when I feel my world's been torn apart.
You are there to help me right from the start.
My soul can reach any days.
I love you more than words can describe.
With all the pain I may gain you help me lose.
If I was in trouble I know you would help me survive.
When I'm feeling down you always seem to bring me up high.
If the day feels dull you make it come alive.
I always shall love you more than the height of the sky.

Vijdan Rasit (13)
Abbey Wood School, Abbey Wood

Love Is Not Something You Can Buy

(Inspired by 'How Do I Love Thee? Let Me Count The Ways' by Elizabeth Barrett Browning)

How much do I love you? Let me count the ways.
I love you to the bottom of my heart to the depths of my soul
My heart glows like dim candlelight in a deep hole
The end of being an idol to your shadow
I love you to the extent of every day
My love for you is just too strong
I've been loving you for just too long
My heart praises you like a non-stop banging drum
I love you like a fire burning deeply in my heart
My pains and passion for you is like a childhood memory
Hiding deep inside me
My love for you is like a never-ending journey to the island of love
On a pushable cart
My love for you can never shame my pride
I can't pretend to act normal when I see you
For the love I share for you is something I can't hide.

Adedolapo Owoseni (12)
Abbey Wood School, Abbey Wood

My One True Love

I love you like the sun burns bright
As if you miss me through the night
When I think of you
I know it's true

I now know that I believe
I love you so much I can't even breathe
I love you with all my heart
I hope we never fall apart

With your bright blue eyes
It looks like the morning skies
When we start to lock
My heart starts to tick like a clock

As soon as I look at you
It will always be me and you.

Ronnie McCarthy (13)
Abbey Wood School, Abbey Wood

Blue . . .

Blue is the sky
With the sun shining bright
Blue makes me feel like telling a lie
Blue can be a magnificent sight.

Blue makes me think of bubblegum
That is chewy and soft
All different flavours that are all really yum
Blue should not be hidden away in a loft.

Blue makes me think of a cold winter's day
When the floor is covered in flakes and snow
As they fall to the ground and lay
Blue is when I'm feeling low.

Blue reminds me of a bluebell
With a story that it can never tell.

Hannah Fitzgerald (13)
Abbey Wood School, Abbey Wood

I Wanna Be Yours

Let me be your honey pot
to sweeten up your day
let me be your household cleaner
to freshen up your way
if you like your ice cream cold
I will make you big and bold
I wanna be yours.

Let me be your tweetie pie
and I will send you sky-high
let me be your fairy godmother
so I can give you wishes
let me be your micro chief
so I can dish you up funky fishes
I wanna be yours.

Let me be your sugar plum
to cover up your little hand
let me be your working bank
so then I can keep safe your big one pound.

Georgia Brooks
Abbey Wood School, Abbey Wood

My Love

Every time we meet
You make my heart skip a beat
When we dance together
It makes me feel like I want to carry on forever
Every time I close my eyes
I think of you and my baby too
You're my love and I will always want to be with you
My love, you make me fearful
Never leave me, that would be evil
I shall never live life without you
I'm so stuck on you, like superglue.

George Watson (13)
Abbey Wood School, Abbey Wood

War

One day in the war,
Someone started a fight,
Some were poor,
This wasn't a pretty sight.

People getting ripped apart,
It wasn't good to look,
And blood getting used as art,
While using one hook.

Now the war is over,
We should celebrate,
Our enemies will be befriended,
We will always mark the date.

We should all think in the future,
Something special to a friend.

Leanne Russell (12) & Sophie Billie-Jo Izzett Harlen (13)
Abbey Wood School, Abbey Wood

Graceful Creature

The graceful creature,
That glides across the lake,
The most beautiful feature,
Ripples in the water she does make.

Her wings are widely spread,
Her beak, orange as the sunset,
Collecting twigs for her bed,
Her soul is free - never a pet.

Her feathers, white as snow,
Sweeps along with her flat, webbed feet,
The colour of her does glow,
Eternal love for her mate when they meet.

She is a swan, queen of the lake,
Like the white icing on top of the cake.

Anne Smith (12)
Abbey Wood School, Abbey Wood

Love

Love is a lie
It makes you snappy
Sometimes you can cry
Then you feel happy

Love can be exciting
Love can be a thing you love
Sometimes it can be inviting
It can be pure, like a dove

Love is beautiful, it can make you full
It can be a wonderful thing
You always answer when I call
You are like my king

The wonders of love cannot be explained
It makes your soul become enflamed.

Muna Rashid (13)
Abbey Wood School, Abbey Wood

Friends

What is it for someone to be your friend?
Someone who can feel your fears
Someone who can understand
And who can wipe your tears.

But if he is not the person you expect,
If he doesn't care anymore,
If he doesn't know the meaning of the word 'respect'
Then just leave him, don't endure.

The real friend will never make you cry,
The real friend will never leave you alone,
The real friend never asks you, 'Why?'
But he is always at the end of the phone.

The best friend is always part of your heart
Like a work of art.

Radost Marinova (13)
Abbey Wood School, Abbey Wood

Football

When we heard the whistle blow,
Then we saw the ref,
That was what we needed to know,
He must be blind and deaf.

All the action that we saw,
We would howl and cheer,
Every time we thought they'd score,
We'd cover our eyes with fear.

Now and again my team will lose,
But they will take it on the chin,
I know what score line I would choose,
When the reds had a 5-4 win.

When the game is finished and done,
We all agree it's the greatest fun.

Andy Lucas (13)
Abbey Wood School, Abbey Wood

Love

Love is all I can give to you,
Two in love can make it and take it,
Love is more than a game for two,
But please don't break my heart and fake it.

Love is a beautiful thing,
Love always comes from the heart,
It will lead you like a string,
Like a work of art.

Love is so pure,
That life is all about love,
You can always be sure,
When you say the word above.

When I hear the word love it makes me feel alive,
Like a soul that has just found it's divine.

Amanda Lakiss (12)
Abbey Wood School, Abbey Wood

I Wanna Be Yours

Let me be your fragrance to make you smell nice
Let me be your flowerpot that shines when the sun's hot
Let me be your chocolate chip cookies with your milk
Let me be your darling, let me be your duvet that keeps you warm

Let me be your clothes to make you look smarter
If you like your chocolate hot, let me be your cream to whisk you right away

Let me be your apple pie, the taste will take you sky high
Let me be your shining star, to shine your true beauty right away
I wanna be yours, not his, for you my darling love,
You are the one that rocks the world around me!
Let me be your sugar in your tea, to melt you right away
And to sail with you in your harmonious dreams.

I wanna be yours forever!

Fatmata Kamara
Abbey Wood School, Abbey Wood

I Wanna Be Yours

Let me be your shoeshine so you will look nice and shiny.
Let me be your hankie to wipe away your tears.
If you like your back to be rubbed, let me be your oil.
If you like your bed to stay warm, let me be your heater.
If you like your skin to be soft, let me be your cream.
Let me be your jewellery shop, let me give you bling.
Let me be your sparkler to lighten up your life.
Let me be your charm to bring you good luck.
Let me be your trolley to carry all your bags.
If you like your chocolate hot, let me be your chocolate pot.
If you like your dishes washed, let me be your washing-up liquid.
If you like to smell nice let me be your perfume.

I don't wanna be his
I wanna be yours.

Ronni Nash
Abbey Wood School, Abbey Wood

I Wanna Be Yours

Let me be your handkerchiefs
to wipe away your tears.
Let me be your jumper
to make you warm when cold.
If you like your perfumes
let me be your rosy flower.
I wanna be yours.

Let me be your umbrella
to make you stay dry.
Let me be your sugar in the tea
to make your tea taste nice.
Let me be your sofa
to make your seat soft.
I don't care what you want,
I wanna be yours.

Let me be your glasses
to make you see better.
Let me be your sweetie pie
to make you feel good.
Let me be your birthday cake,
I will blow out your candles.
Let me be your shiny star
to make you feel joy in your life.
If you love your money
let me be your bank.
I wanna be yours.

Let me be your water
to make you feel fresh every time.
Let me be your warrior
to make you stay safe from danger.
Let me be the one to give you everything you need.
I want to be with you.
I have deep emotions for you,
very deep emotions and feelings.
I don't want to lose you (baby),
I wanna be yours.

Oluwafisayo Osiewu-Seriki
Abbey Wood School, Abbey Wood

Aim

I wanna be your pen
To write your own poem
Let me be your lie detector
I will never die
Let me be your foot massager
I will never break
Let me be your sweet Malteser
I will never melt
I wanna be yours.

Let me be your lunch at work
I will always be there
Let me be your Ford Cortina
I will take you everywhere
Let me be your pen and paper
Wherever you are
Sooner or later I will love you forever and ever
I wanna be yours.

Let me be your vacuum cleaner
Sucking in your worries of life
Let me be your apple pie
My taste might send you higher than high
Let me be your pillow at night
To wear off those weary nights
Let me be your heart of emotion
I will not break
I don't wanna be hers
I wanna be yours.

Rushdien Basardien (12)
Abbey Wood School, Abbey Wood

I Wanna Be Yours

Let me be your star at night
Let me make you shine so bright
Let me be your sleeping pillow
While we watch the weeping willow
If you like your tea hot
I will be your honey pot
I wanna be yours

Let me be your sweetheart
I will be your dancing dart
Let me be your cherry pie
Let me go sky high
If you like the way I smile
I will be your love card pile.

Let me be your dolly girl
I will have my hair in a curl
Let me be your jewellery box
I won't let you have chickenpox
If you love me
I love you more than a buzz from a bee
I wanna be yours.

Victoria Morris (12)
Abbey Wood School, Abbey Wood

I Don't Wanna Be Yours

I don't wanna be yours
because you flirt with other boys
I don't wanna be yours
because you eat like a pig
if you want me
then you'll have to work harder
I don't wanna be yours
because you don't do any housework
I call the shots
I don't wanna be yours
I don't wanna be yours
because I do all the cooking
I don't wanna be yours
because you don't do the washing
I don't wanna be yours
because I do the cleaning
I don't care
I don't wanna be yours
I don't wanna be yours
because you don't talk to me
I don't wanna be yours
because you keep secrets
I don't wanna be yours
because I don't love you
I don't care
you're dumped!

Kallan Breeds
Abbey Wood School, Abbey Wood

I Wanna Be Yours!

Let me be your cooker
So you can rest your tired feet,
Let me be your server
When you are beat
If you like your chocolate
Let me be your chocolate melting in your mouth
You can stay up late
I wanna be yours.

Let me be your jam pie
Filling you with delicious taste
Let me be your swing
To swing you up high
If you like your coffee sweet
Let me be your sweetener
I don't care
I wanna be yours.

Let me be your fireplace
So I can keep you warm throughout the night
Let me be your teddy bear
So you can cuddle me anywhere
If you like your clothes soft
Let me be your softener
I don't wanna be his
I wanna be yours.

Amy-Louise Hutchings (12)
Abbey Wood School, Abbey Wood

I Wanna Be Yours

Let me be your sweetheart when you open the door
Let me be your fluffy pillow to wipe out all your sorrow
If you like your clothes clean
Let me be your washing machine
I wanna be yours.

Let me be your teddy bear, that way you will not have nightmares
Let me be your roses in a vase so you can smell me when you go past
Let me teach you love, so forever and ever it can just be us
How about you and me, I'll look after you, don't you worry
I wanna be yours.

If you're in pain I will take it for you over and over again
When you're out in the sun I will be your suntan lotion
I love you with so much emotion
How about you take this love potion
I wanna be yours.

Let me be your smoke alarm so I can keep you protected
Please - I don't want to be rejected
Let me be your bluebird in the tree, so when it sings you will think of
me
I don't wanna be his
I wanna be yours.

Inderpal Bhachu
Abbey Wood School, Abbey Wood

Storm

Rain, wind, air and fire
Clouds, thunder and lightning
Through the air is striking
A giant storm of desire

The rain is flooding higher
The storm puts out the lightning
A risen fury as it is fighting
Tornado like a flying wire

Twisting, turning tornadoes
Striking, glowing lightning
Hard, heavy hail

Snow like falling potatoes
The mass cyclone tightening
Anything can easily fail

Soon the world goes
But the human race keeps on fighting

The rain is coming like a hose
The storm needs a better sighting

It begins with that first snowflake on the nose
The cold skin whitening.

Adam Gates (12)
Abbey Wood School, Abbey Wood

Love

Love is so pure,
It comes from the heart,
You cannot stop once it starts,
It can be a lovely cure.

Hate is the opposite, it's like a big sore,
You should never hate,
You should not debate,
You should only adore.

You should never just close the door,
You should always keep a clean slate,
On your first date,
Your love can be so secure.

Marie Brennan
Abbey Wood School, Abbey Wood

Year By Year

In winter the snowflakes fall and drift along the sea;
Glistening, shimmering, shining, falling on me;
They make the world so peaceful, delicate and calm;
Falling, covering everything, I feel safe and out of harm.

In spring when the birds begin, again, to sing to me;
So beautiful and calming as the blossom from a tree;
The flowers which then bloom - attract a bumblebee;
Buzzing around the pretty flowers and colours I can see.

In summer with the shining sun I feel like someone new;
The happiness it brings makes me smile too;
Laying on a hot day with such a wonderful sight;
Watching the sun on the sea, twinkling, shining bright.

In autumn as the leaves fall, I love to hear them crunch;
Walking through a park you can hear the squirrels munch;
The orange, reds and browns with the hazy autumn sun;
These are all the seasons I love, each and every one!

Emma Morton (14)
Archbishop Tenison's CE High School, Croydon

What Am I?

I uncover the truth yet conceal it too
What am I?
I have seen Man's greatest invention destroy cities at the blink
of an eye
What am I?
I live through the darkest of me
What am I?
I have seen an evil oppressor lead a simple country to war and be
defeated by agents of the Devil portrayed as heroes
What am I?
I never end but am always ageing
What am I?
I have seen Man's greed lead him to consume himself
What am I?
I am there at the beginning and at the end
What am I?
No weapon will ever blemish me
What am I? What am I?

Time.

Myles Manyonda (13)
Archbishop Tenison's CE High School, Croydon

Family Holiday

Past the border, now there's no return
the long fortnight has just begun
the classic melodies drown on and on
the tatty caravan bounds along
no escape from the heat
no way out!
Trapped . . . in the point of no return
isolated in a world of our own.

No escape!

Harriet Smith (14)
Archbishop Tenison's CE High School, Croydon

Dreams

Confusing, deceiving,
amazing but shocking,
magical,
where you can touch but cannot feel,
even though it looks so real,
you feel as if you are lost,
you cannot get out,
you're trapped.

They are beautiful,
they lie,
and are extremely strange,
bad things transform to good,
you cannot believe them,
but you are drawn in,
dazzling, deceiving,
taking every emotion,
tricking you,
stealing your thoughts,
you are between what is and what seems.

Danielle Homer (13)
Archbishop Tenison's CE High School, Croydon

Harry's Imagination

H arry is my name
A ggravating I can be
R ush, rush, rush, I can't sit still
'R ude' is what the adults say.
Y awning, do I have to behave?

B e good, I tell myself
U nderpants I wear as Superman
N obody understands my humour.
N o one at all.

Harry Bunn (12)
Archbishop Tenison's CE High School, Croydon

Or Would I?

Pedestrianism, 1, 2, 1, 2,
The build-up to dying,
My friends lined up,
Would they still be there
When I'm surrounded by Germans?
When I'm left for dead in no-man's-land?
Will they come to get me?
I mean, they've got to,
I would for them,
Bullets flying over my head,
Bombshells spraying all around me,
The bayonets shining on the opposite side of the field,
Or would I?
I've lost so many,
There's not many left,
The front line's scary,
The Somme was the worst,
I was one of the few that survived,
The massacre was sickly,
I wanted to save my friends,
However the explosion was too powerful,
Mustard gas is deadly,
But chlorine gas is just pure brutal,
That's how my friends died,
They suffocated,
I had to sit there and watch,
As my friends grabbed me,
As if they wanted me to do something,
I wanted to,
Believe me.

Daniel Turner (14)
Archbishop Tenison's CE High School, Croydon

Pain

I open my eyes
The pain is back
Trying to escape
My mind is black

Can't get away
From the terrible pain
Consciousness
Is what I need to gain

I scream in agony
No one hears my cry
My pain is my company
Torture and I

I feel I'm trapped
And all alone
My head is in darkness
My heart is stone

I reach out, trembling
Take my hand
Someone, anyone
You must understand

All is silent
Excruciating pain
Lies within me
I close my eyes again.

Stephanie Wood (14)
Archbishop Tenison's CE High School, Croydon

What An Influence

What an influence,
It gets you through pressure,
It gets you through pain,
What an influence,
It inspires you,
It teaches you new things,
What an influence,
It shows you originality,
It shows you talent,
What an influence,
It comes in different forms,
Different people like different forms,
What an influence,
It's playable at different levels,
Some people don't like the high levels,
Don't listen to them,
Do what you feel like,
What an influence it makes,
Music is all around us,
But we don't quite know,
What an influence music can be.

David Marley (14)
Archbishop Tenison's CE High School, Croydon

Chelsea Is My Team

Blue is the colour
Chelsea is my team
We're fired up together
To win every game in the league.

Roman Abramovich
Money in the bag
We've got brill players
Like super Frankie Lampard.

Top corner of the net
Gudjohnson once again
Goal of the month
It definitely had a bend.

Round the wall
From the free kick taker
'Cause Chelsea
Chelsea is my team.

Makelele holds the back
He does it every game
Terry is the captain
To get us through the match.

So cheer us on
Through the sun and rain
'Cause Chelsea
Chelsea is my team.

Matt Rolfe (14)
Archbishop Tenison's CE High School, Croydon

Poem

In the midst of war, dark and grey
I feel trapped in a cruel game that God is starting to play.
I feel scared, frightened, I really want out
But all I can do is scream and shout.
It's not fair, it isn't, what did I do to deserve this?
Oh God, a grenade on the ground starts to hiss,
So I run for my life, not daring to look back,
Whilst I run I think of my good friend, Jack,
And all the pain he suffered in his short life,
21 years of pain, anguish, trouble and strife.
But then it all came to an abrupt stop,
Poor Jack was gunned down by a stupid cop.
Completely innocent, he died straight away,
On the thirtieth day in the month of May.
I pray for him, then dodge a huge blast,
That soldier shot that missile fast.
The taste of gunpowder lingers in my mouth.
I can see my comrades die on the ground,
Blood foaming from their lips.
Then I decide to avenge my friends' deaths,
By shooting and blasting off my enemies' heads.
Without a care in the world, my life has been hell.
Just as I feel I've won and beaten the best,
A searing pain enters my chest.
I've been shot by those evil tykes,
So this is what dying feels like,
Amazingly it doesn't feel so bad.
Then I black out and never wake up.
My soul departs from my mangled body,
And rises up to the heavens.

Greg Lee (14)
Archbishop Tenison's CE High School, Croydon

Fire And Ash

Mountains of rock,
Towering high,
Fuming and flaming,
Preparing to blow,
Then deadly events,
Are unleashed from its brim.
The fiery colossus,
Overwhelmingly high,
Devastation and danger, released from its bowels.
Blistering heat,
Mighty explosions,
Staggering destruction,
All unleashed from these lumps of rock.
Pernicious ash,
Shot up from the base,
Rains down from the heavens
Chokes the land and all who dwell.
Its red-hot spittle,
Ejected eternally,
Charring the land,
Scorching the ground,
Destroying everything it touches.
All of this,
From mountains of rock,
Towering high,
Fuming and flaming,
Preparing to blow.

Justin Hill (14)
Archbishop Tenison's CE High School, Croydon

Haikus

Trust is . . .
Trust is assurance
Trust is faith, hope and sureness
Trust is certainty.

Help is . . .
Help is guidance and
Help is aid and support and
Help is to succour.

Hope is . . .
Hope is ambition
Hope is aspiration and
Hope is the future.

Fame is . . .
Fame is majesty
Fame is an acclamation
Fame is recognised.

Death is . . .
Death is the darkness
Death is the curtains falling
Death is departure.

Alice Howard (13)
Archbishop Tenison's CE High School, Croydon

The Secret Little Man

The secret little man hides away in a hole,
No one knows he's there,
Not even the man with a mole,
He really doesn't care,
He enjoys being by himself,
He likes being greedy and spending all his wealth,
Every day a giant foot passes,
And he laughs with glee,
That they don't know he's there,
However he is yet to see,
That this greedy man is lonely,
Deep down he is sad,
Soon he will become frustrated and eventually go mad,
Then he hears a knock on the door,
And he doesn't know but his happiness will grow more,
It's another secret little man,
Who comes in peace and brought his nan,
He said, 'Hello, nice to meet you, my name is Bobby Lou.'
Both of them became best friends and Bob moved in too.
'I was always too scared to see you, my nan said stay away.'
Now the secret man had just discovered a lie he believed his whole life,
He wasn't a secret man at all,
Now he feels extra tall.

Katrina Kedwards (13)
Archbishop Tenison's CE High School, Croydon

Before Dreams

Death of the light
As day becomes night
That's when the darkness comes

Death of the light
It's with me tonight
It makes me feel alone

Death of the light
It obscures my sight
And the shadows come to play

Death of the light
I don't feel alright
As the silence fills the air

Death of the light
As the black sheet takes flight
Moon and stars pierce through

Death of the light
I shut my eyes tight
And fall asleep.

Josh Bates (14)
Archbishop Tenison's CE High School, Croydon

The End Of School

The echo of the school bell vibrates through the corridor,
The teacher declares the end of school,
And two words enter the pupils' ears,
'Pack up.'
Chairs rumble, zips open and close as bags swallow books,
'Class dismissed.'
The classroom door is swung open,
Nearly ripped off its hinges,
A stampede of students rush out of classrooms,
And shake the building,
Lockers slam shut and padlocks close,
They keep the world of PE kits, coats and books safe,
Pupils practically fly out of school,
Wanting to get home fast,
Bus stops are crowded and traffic is endless,
Cars start their engines, completing the school run,
Swarms of kids rummage in their pockets for money, saver
tickets or bus passes,
They long to catch the early bus,
Other children jump into cars, hoping to miss the traffic,
Journeys begin and all is calm,
But then they get home and realise . . .
That they have to do it all again tomorrow.

Rebecca Palmer (13)
Archbishop Tenison's CE High School, Croydon

Our Memories

Remember, remember the 5th of November
Remember, remember the last of December

Remember, remember my birthday
With a big chocolate cake reading 'Happy Birthday'

Remember, remember Easter day
When Jesus rose again from the tomb in which he'd laid

Remember the day when your dad got promoted,
He bought a new Game Boy, but now it's just broken

Remember the day on your aunty's wedding
All dressed in white, and the bridesmaids in lemon

These are all memories that everyone has every day or every hour
Whether you're sweet or whether you're sour.

Azelia Aqui (14)
Archbishop Tenison's CE High School, Croydon

What A Bore . . .

Homework, what a bore
Something about history's blood and gore
Maths makes my brain sore
My standards are poor
English, um, what can I say?
Just no more of Shakespeare's play
'How do you spell?' 'What?' 'Not sure'
Oh science! *Give me more!*
German, oh what a bore!
Teaching it should be against the law
But there is some hope
Something left, I think, maybe
Some lessons well they're such a bore
Others they're simply, encore! Encore!

David Moseley (14)
Archbishop Tenison's CE High School, Croydon

The Screen

I can see a screen right in front of me.
I can see a screen brightly.
It could be big and tall.
It is very colourful.
The best part is when it plays my favourite things.
I like my screen, it plays all my films.
I can see a screen right in front of me.
It's my favourite thing.
I look at it every week.
24 hours a day, 7 days a week.
I have seen the screen for 2 years running.
I can't wait until the new film's coming.
I think about it every day.
It is the very best thing.
I like the screen, it is the thing.

Travis Spruit (13)
Archbishop Tenison's CE High School, Croydon

Jemz Haikus

Love is beautiful
Love is consistently true;
Love never ever fails.

Hate is uncaring,
Hate is blasphemous always;
Hate is arrogant.

Truth is rejoicing,
Truth is excruciating;
Truth, glad all over.

Faith is thinking hard,
Faith, believing not seeing;
Faith is amazing.

Apathy is half,
Apathy is near enough;
Apathy is 'cool'.

Jeremy Stevens (14)
Archbishop Tenison's CE High School, Croydon

Snow And Ice

The sun reflecting off the ice
The sun glistening in the brightness
Children skating, slipping over
Magnificent pure white all around

Cold and misty lakes everywhere
People fishing to survive
Storms overhead making shadows on the snow
Gigantic mountains towering high

Beautiful nature growing and living
All the colours of the rainbow
Beetles crawling and eagles soaring
Every object becomes alive

Glaciers meandering through the valleys
Children playing in the snow
Every eye at last can see
The beauty of the frozen land.

David Clark (13)
Archbishop Tenison's CE High School, Croydon

Grandma's Love

G randma from the top of her head to the soles of her feet is . . .
R esponsible and demonstrative,
A ccomplished and constructive,
N ectarines are her favourite fruit and
D ressing up is her favourite game. Early
M orning, Gran's not in bed, she says, 'Sleep
A ll day and it'll hurt your head.'
S ome people say their grandmas are too strict or too nosy,
but my grandma is just right.

L ater on, Grandma and I find pleasure looking
O ver the glittering sea, listening to Grandma speaking words
of wisdom to me
'V alue your life and always be the best you can be'
E ach word Grandma tells me I will always remember.

Jessika Downes-Gössl (12)
Archbishop Tenison's CE High School, Croydon

Tidy It Now!

'There's no point as it will just get messy again.'
'Mum, my head hurts, I'm in so much pain.'
'There's no space to put all of this junk.'
'It's not as bad as Ben's, his smells like a skunk.'
'I will do it tomorrow, if I'm not busy.'
'No sorry, got to straighten my hair, it's frizzy.'
'Why don't you do it? It's your house.'

'There is a point, your clothes are on the floor.'
'People would be amazed at the mess, and like a tour.'
'Your room smells or worse than an animal.'
'Smells like left-over food from a cannibal.'
'Do it now, it's your home too.'
'I'm not letting you do it tomorrow, I'm not cuckoo.'
'So get to it, now, make sure it's clean.'
'Spick, span, tidy and sheen.'

Carine Packer (14)
Archbishop Tenison's CE High School, Croydon

Hair

Long hair
Short hair
Somewhere in-between hair

Neat hair
Scruffy hair
Orange, red and blue hair

My hair
Your hair
The person over there's hair

Chest hair
Head hair
Dog hair

Yuck
Nose hair!

Abigail Bates (12)
Archbishop Tenison's CE High School, Croydon

Suddenly I Start To Shrink

Suddenly I start to shrink
Heart thumping like a giant
How did this happen?
Did I eat too many sweets?
My stomach roaring like a lion
Or a volcano erupting
I'm getting lower to the ground
World looking down at me
Now I'm as tiny as a
Small coffee table now a
Kettle, this is my worst nightmare
And still getting smaller
I can feel my legs getting weaker
And still getting smaller
Now I feel I'm going to disappear
Now I'm as small as a
Grain of sand on a beach!

Natalie Card (12)
Archbishop Tenison's CE High School, Croydon

The Weather's Like A Feather

Oh tiresome, dreary rain,
in my life, this is a pain,
and the snow,
which lies below,
puts me on a natural low,
and that horrible breeze,
which makes me wheeze,
and the dust like hail,
which will forever flail,
but then the sunlight hits the sky,
and puts my soul on a natural high.

Alex McLaughlin (14)
Archbishop Tenison's CE High School, Croydon

Forest Treasure

I crunched through the forest that day
To find your glamorous roots
The decrepit leaves lay there dead,
Their metamorphosis almost complete

I shuffled through the crumpled flowers,
Their heads scattered far
Lying in the naked clearing
Acaulescent daises surrounding me

I wandered through the myriad of trees
Backed by a pastiche of birds
I brushed through the undergrowth
And spotted the twist of your glorious trunk

I danced through the dappled sunlight
Bathing in your gravitas presence
Your awesome perennial bark
Dazzling my pusillanimous soul

I stroked your mature branches
Wrinkled complexion, yet so young
The logorrhoea of monkeys
Nibbling at your sun-kissed juicy fruits

I climbed your recherché great canopy
Silent. Mythical. Radiant,
Surveying the vast forest grounds
Relaxing in your tender, loving arms.

Melanie Goodwin (13)
Archbishop Tenison's CE High School, Croydon

I Will *Always* Remember Her

I will always remember her,
She always comforted me
She told me it was okay,
She'd take my hands,
I will never forget her.

I will always remember her,
As she soothed my pain
She held me tight,
She'd always forgive me if I did wrong.

I will always remember her,
Her wise sayings
This made me think
When she told me off I knew she loved me
It's impossible to forget

Now she is gone
I will remember all that she said,
I know that she is watching over me
And she will be waiting until we meet again
I love my mum very much.

Samantha Fletcher (13)
Archbishop Tenison's CE High School, Croydon

The Forest

Shrivelled leaves, green leaves,
Burnt umber leaves and brown leaves.

Great trees towering high into the air,
Keeping sinister watch upon below,
Ominous and threatening.

Shady hollows,
Concealing what lies inside,
Harbouring hidden dangers and dark secrets.

Twisted roots span the gloom-filled ground,
Mangled and twisted,
Grasping snares set to trap.

Creatures scurry all around,
Creatures gnawing, scraping and yelping,
Their whole world completely unknown and unseen.

Flowers dot the sodden ground,
Exquisite flares of colour,
Bringing light to the dark floor.

Waterfalls sparkle,
Tumbling, gushing and cascading,
Into shimmering glassy pools.

Stuart Davis (13)
Archbishop Tenison's CE High School, Croydon

Beaches

The warm sand sparkles in the sun
The cool sea glistens in the light
The smooth sand sinks beneath your feet
As the sun glows and all becomes night

The crystal clear sea
Translucent as the air
The warm, cool waters in the Caribbean ocean
Meticulous sights embark on us all
The shallow waters of the Maldives
As the people experience the sight

I love the beach
I go there thrice a year
I relax on the luscious sand
And walk along the pier

Beaches are great
Beaches are calm
Beaches are extravagant
Beaches are calm.

Patrick Miller (14)
Archbishop Tenison's CE High School, Croydon

Our Love

The first day we met,
No time to neglect,
Only time to reflect
On our love where our eyes were set.
My eyes were set on his charming face,
I could not wait to embrace
Or meet again in that special place.

It wasn't a quick crush
Because I wasn't willing to rush or brush,
His love or his lovely touch,
But to continue to stay,
With all the things coming on that blissful day.

Our love felt eternal,
Like there would never be an end to the tunnel,
Never ending, never bending.

But our love turned sour,
Couldn't stand seeing each other another hour,
We began to part ways.
We forgot about all those special days,
And our memories that we share.
Our love for each other we could no longer bear.

Our love was becoming history.
Never ending for eternity
Our love went through a struggle
We met the end of the tunnel.
It started ending.
Continually bending.
Our blissful days were over
He was no longer my lover.

Esther Appiagyei (13)
Archbishop Tenison's CE High School, Croydon

Fighting Against War!

How does war start?
Who starts it?
Why does it end with war?
Would you like to fight?
Why can't we make peace?

The streets are not safe
War against drugs
Gangs beating each other up
Causing each other pain and hurt
Cursing and wearing

Stop the wars and fighting
Killing and dying
Slaughtering and suffering
Stop this madness
Fighting doesn't settle anything
Does it make you feel good?

Gunshots everywhere
Loads of explosions and shouting
A never-ending river of blood
And piles of bodies

Why can't we make peace?
. . . *World peace*
War hurts
Stop the fighting
And make peace.

Jack Coles (12)
Archbishop Tenison's CE High School, Croydon

When I Was So Much Younger

When I was so much younger,
My imagination was wild,
I used to play around a lot,
When I was just a child.

I used to take a wire,
And wrap it round my ear,
Then bend it forward, like a mic,
And I was Britney Spears!

I put on shows for family,
Nearly every day,
Always full of dances,
Some hour-long plays.

My sister was my co-star,
Always by my side,
But I *always* played the princess,
No matter how she cried.

When I was so much younger,
My imagination was wild,
I used to play around a lot,
When I was just a child.

Nicola Blackman (14)
Archbishop Tenison's CE High School, Croydon

Seasons Haikus

Bees on the flowers,
Chicks coming out at Easter
Oh, the joy of spring.

Hot sun, sea and sand,
Water fights in September,
Ice creams all summer.

Bare branches on trees,
Fireworks and Hallowe'en,
Colours of the wind.

Snow landing on trees,
The trees sway like skeletons,
Santa Claus has come.

Summer and autumn,
And all the joy that they bring,
Just to hear birds sing.

Spring follows winter,
The blue sky instead of grey,
A breath of fresh air.

Emily Layton (14)
Archbishop Tenison's CE High School, Croydon

Golf

Golf, one of my favourite sports,
The relaxing peace and quiet of green paradise,
And the birds singing joyfully in the trees,
A massive valley which seems like it's all to yourself,
A glorious view across the whole course,
Under a hot summer's sun,
In a clear sky,
As I hit the ball, a soft ping sounds,
And the ball soars through the air,
Slicing the air out of its way,
Like a hot knife cutting butter.
Then it drops like a small meteor,
Surging towards the ground.

Edmund Cooper (13)
Archbishop Tenison's CE High School, Croydon

Theseus And The Minotaur

The cold, dripping, spooky maze
Frightens me like a nightmare.
Murky halls make me feel cramped.
Screams echo like a ringing bell.
Razor-sharp teeth, blood, death,
Horrifying thoughts whiz through my head.
Darkness is all I see.
I trudge along, slowly, slowly.
Waiting, walking, strange, weird creatures crawl over me.
Footsteps quietly hit the rough surface.
All of a sudden the ground is shaking,
A huge figure is approaching me.
Completely scared, I march towards it,
Green bulging eyes are staring, staring,
The monster seems calm,
But without warning I get a huge scar, 4 lines on my chest.
Frightened, I start to fight . . .

Benjamin Edwards-Wilks (12)
Archbishop Tenison's CE High School, Croydon

Family

As I tell this to you, I am weeping,
Please don't tell anyone,
I love my family dearly,
Brother, Dad and Mum.

They embarrass for a laugh,
But sometimes not for fun,
I want to forgive them,
But what they did has been done.

I have a weight on my shoulders,
Something pushing me down,
Not a happy face in sight,
Just droopy eyes and frowns.

I love it when they're happy,
And there is a smile on their face,
But I *hate* it when they shout and swear,
When we're in a public place.

When we get home there'll be shouting,
Then hugs and kisses for all,
But will the people in that public place forgive us
Or will we look like the local fools?

Immy Brown (12)
Archbishop Tenison's CE High School, Croydon

Climbing Up A Mountain

Now I've climbed up this emotional mountain,
I've been here for 5 months, nearly 6.
All of a sudden when everything is OK,
I find myself back at the bottom again.
Making a flowing river of tears,
I'm hurting inside, a sharp pain.
But someone's still here, holding my hand,
Ready to show the way again.
And I'm gonna keep a-climbing up that mountain.
I start to climb again,
Someone's helping, showing the way.
There's all the spiky rocks again.
But knowing I need to find my way,
And not stay at the bottom.
And I'm gonna keep a-climbing up that mountain.
My life isn't over.
All I need is someone,
Someone to stitch up my bleeding, broken heart.
To tell me they love and show me the way.
I won't give up,
I'm gonna keep a-climbing up that mountain!

Megan Eager (12)
Archbishop Tenison's CE High School, Croydon

Doors Wide Open

City smashed,
Hope destroyed,
Doors wide open,
Troops deployed.

Defend the gate,
Rally to the call,
Doors wide open,
Killers all.

Stand and shoot,
Clashing steel,
Doors wide open,
Fate is sealed.

Barricade up,
Won't last long,
Doors wide open,
To the evil throng.

Horns of triumph,
Galloping hooves,
Doors wide open,
Hilltop moves.

Hordes of riders,
Charging spear,
Doors wide open,
Help is here.

Two great cities,
Safe at last,
Doors wide open,
Like ancient past.

Stuart Cottrell (11)
Archbishop Tenison's CE High School, Croydon

The Dream

England went to Portugal, a hyped-up team,
To win the Championship was Beckham's dream.
They played a few friendlies to keep them in tune,
A couple of wins and Sven was over the moon.
Well came the day, their first big game,
Against France, to win was their aim.
England scored first and it wasn't luck,
But France scored two, England came unstuck.
The second game was against the Swiss,
This was a game we dare not miss.
England had to win or they would be on the plane,
But their fears were laid to rest by a lad named Wayne.
Things looked better, a win was on the cards,
Then to make sure, along came Gerrard.
Sven says their next effort would be even greater,
That will show when they meet Croatia.
The game wasn't easy, but it wasn't a bore,
Croatia scored two but England scored four.
So on to the next game, it looked a breeze,
Our opponents were the hosts, the Portuguese.
Hopes were high when Owen scored,
In only three minutes we had a goal on the board.
Then the hosts scored, the game was all square,
The ninety minutes were nearly there.
The game was heading for extra time,
The silver goal was on the line.
Well extra time started and the hosts scored again,
But Lampard struck which pleased our Sven.
Penalties were surely on the cards,
The worry on the takers is very hard.
The players stepped up to take their turn,
Sad to say we missed two, Portugal had won.

The dream was over . . .

Michael Boateng (13)
Archbishop Tenison's CE High School, Croydon

The Day I Won't Forget

You taught me once
but I forgot all
the friend you ever were
to care, smile and to
always be there for me
I remember when you hugged
and kissed me
and all the good days we had,
moments with you
where nobody else was
to care, kiss away tears
and bring smiles on rainy days
to listen to my problems.

You were there when I lost
the one and only
. . . my mum . . .
but now I have lost you
I would never ever forget you
the time we had,
the special moment
I'll always remember,
you're in my heart forever,
whenever
. . . forever . . .

Alba Hidalgo (14)
Archbishop Tenison's CE High School, Croydon

Abuse

He comes after me every night and day
even if I try to hide away
he bangs so hard on the door
that I sit and tremble on the floor.
    Eventually he gets in my room
    he starts to chase me
    soon he has hold of me
    has me pinned in a corner
    and that's when his fists attack.
He pounds me so hard I lose my breath
so I fall and wait for my death
but this always happens, it never comes
when he leaves, in comes Mum.
    Monday morning comes
    I can't speak out
    can't bring myself to tell people
    people think I'm fine
    if I just sit and smile.
As I walk home
through an alleyway
it's there that I realise
my life's not worth living.
    I clatter into my bed
    clutching the syringe
    whilst laying there I realise
    if only I'd spoken out
    maybe this abuse
    would be over . . .
    . . . well, it is now.

Adele Warne (14)
Archbishop Tenison's CE High School, Croydon

The Debut Match

Looking at the name
Looking at the number
Pulling up your socks
And slipping on your vapours
Walking out of the changing room
Standing in the tunnel
The roar of the crowd as we enter the pitch
The formation line up
The referee's whistle
Tweeeet!
And the stadium erupts.

The left go to right
Taking it on the half turns
The tracking back
The hunger and desire
The adrenaline rushing through the whole of your body
The set from the striker
The strike into the top corner
The players celebrating, the crowd going wild.

The 92nd minute and the ref with the whistle,
Tweeeet!
And the crowd go ballistic

The manager shaking your hand
Your name in the headlines

Your first professional match
Your first professional goal.

Hakeem Adelakun (14)
Archbishop Tenison's CE High School, Croydon

Knocked Down

The anticipation for my first fight
Was like 10 Christmas Eves rolled into one.
People normally dread it,
But I'm like a Jack Russell,
Playful with a nasty bite.
The build up and the crowd roaring
Filled me with confidence,
However the person opposite
Was tall, well-built and had a nasty reputation.
The first punch was his,
My goodness it hurt,
It sent a pain down my spine,
Like laying on a bed of nails.
I stayed determined,
Focused my power,
I swung and missed.
All this training,
All this work,
I was throwing it away.
He just kept on hitting me,
He was like a machine,
A pitbull,
That wasn't why I was here.
Before I knew it I felt
The sensation of the cushioned floor,
I was out cold,
The 10 count went,
I wasn't prepared!

Daniel Turner (14)
Archbishop Tenison's CE High School, Croydon

Drain Night

A drainpipe is a structure
Sturdy and bold
Supported by bricks
Disrupted by rust
Stands alone in the dark
Dull and discoloured
Decrepit and deformed
Looming in danger
Within the lonely night
The eerie creek approaches
The defective construction
Damp with a drip
Gushing down sides
Frozen through
Corroded with a decomposed centre
Cursed by the night.

Marie Crayden (14)
Archbishop Tenison's CE High School, Croydon

Acrostic Poem

V irgin has all the games.
I t's like playing with toys on TV.
D iving in and out of TV.
E very day, I play every day.
O n-going games to play.

G ames I enjoy playing every day
A t any time of the day.
M akes me relax.
E asy to play.
S uper games to be invented.

Emanuel Lehuede (14)
Bensham Manor School, Thornton Heath

My Mum

My mum is lovely.
I really love her.
She's always there for me.
She cares for me a lot.

She always looks after me when I'm upset.
When I cry, she is a really good shoulder to cry on.

She always does a bum dance in front of me.
It's really embarrassing.
I sometimes do an impression of her doing it too.

She always pulls silly faces at me.
She makes me laugh.

She buys things for me.
She sometimes takes me to the cinema.

She makes me smile.
She makes me laugh.
She makes me cry.

I love her so much.

She makes excellent cakes.
Chocolate cakes.
Yum-yum!

She is an excellent cook.

She has quite a few talents.
She's also a really good singer.

She does everything for me.

Washes my clothes.
Cooks my meals for me.
Looks after me when I'm upset.

She looks after me.
I love her so much,
My mum is the best mum in the world.

Jonathan Mark Land (14)
Bensham Manor School, Thornton Heath

Acrostic Poem

F riendship is important
R eally nice
I go out with my friends
E very outing is fun
N ever a sad day
D ishing out gossip
S o special.

Rachel Attwood (14)
Bensham Manor School, Thornton Heath

Chelsea FC

C helsea are Premiership Champions
H aving waited 50 years for it
E very Chelsea fan loves the colour blue
L osing only one Premiership game to Man City
S uper Frank Lampard scores lots of goals
E nglish players are John Terry and Frank Lampard
A rsenal are losers this year

F antastic celebrations at Stamford Bridge
C hampions 2004 to 2005 season.

Luke Harvey (13)
Bensham Manor School, Thornton Heath

Acrostic Poem

L ovely person
O nly has eyes for me
V ery happy all the time
E specially when he sees me
R omantic
S o lucky he is with me.

Bonita Christian Gray (13)
Bensham Manor School, Thornton Heath

My Little Big Brother

The bump has landed, oh what a wait
He arrived at last, ten days late.

His life started out like any other child,
He was sweet, innocent and he was mild.
As the months travelled on, time seemed to fly,
And his height was aiming straight for the sky.

The force of his feet continued to grow,
Until an Olympic runner was considered slow.
His mouth grew so big, people would stop and stare,
His speeches were ace, better than Tony Blair.

His mind was bigger than Einstein himself,
So he wrote tonnes of books which are now on the shelf.
His cereal in the morning filled up a bottomless pit,
And every girl in the world considered him fit.

His face was on every channel on TV,
He barely had time to look down on me.
I kept on hoping he'd send me a letter,
But every day his popularity got better.

But he's my little big brother and he can be great,
He's not only my brother, he's my mate.
Sometimes we'd fight like we were in the ring,
But I wouldn't change him, not one single thing!

I can remember playing football and he'd always score,
As you can see this is all incredible, as he's still only four!

Claire Power (13)
Blackheath High School, London

Future Man

My breath shortened
The walls closed in
Although I'd only bruised my shin

Strange things happened
As if the bushes were alive
The roses got married and became husband and wife

Doors slammed repeatedly
The TV switched on
It was 25 past 1 but the bells went dong, dong, dong

The turtle's pace quickened
The leopard turned as slow
As Cancan dancers in slow mo

Rulers lost control
Getting numbers muddled up
A dog appeared from the camel's hump

People stopped
They started to jump
The world turned into a beatbox going bump, bump, bump

I looked around
And there I saw
A madman with an electric saw.

Emily Phillips (11)
Blackheath High School, London

Life's Secrets

Love is a flower,
Always blooming,
Always sharing,
Always caring,
Oh so daring.

Fear is a cage,
Never going,
Never knowing,
Always there,
So unfair.

Hope is a gift,
A star,
A dream,
The most wonderful taste,
Like strawberries and cream.

Death is a ticket,
To Hell,
Or Heaven,
The worst of them all,
Is this mighty call.

Ruby Stevenson (11)
Blackheath High School, London

Where Were You?

Where were you when I was really scared?
I was really frightened then,
I was crying,
My eyes like fountains with tears.
My heart was thumping,
Practically jumping out of my chest.
I was trembling,
I had an earthquake in my body.
I was all alone then,
Where were you?

Where were you when I had just won a race?
I was so happy then,
Really smiling,
So hard it hurt.
I looked around the crowd for you,
Trying to spot your face,
I couldn't see you anywhere,
Like you disappeared without a trace.
I had just won!
Where were you?

Where are you now
When I'm writing this down?
I'm trying not to remember,
All the times you have let me down.
I'm trying to forget you,
Wiping you from my memory,
So I won't be waiting for you ever again.
But I have one last question before I leave you now,
When I was all alone . . .
Where were you?

Miranda Justo-Nunez (12)
Blackheath High School, London

Homework Excuses

'Your homework?'
'Oh, Miss, my dog chewed it this morning.'
'Nonsense, you don't have a dog, Dear.'
'But I do, Miss, I got one last week.'

'Your homework today, children.'
'Well, my printer broke down, Miss.'
'Send it to school, Child.'
'She is so foul and just too formal.'

'Child, your homework.'
'Well, the homework didn't come through, Miss.'
'Well, get your printer fixed.'
'It's getting fixed today.'

'Well?'
'It printed, but the gerbils got their paws on it and chewed it up.'
'Well, why didn't you print it again?'
'Mum says only one copy per homework.'

'Well, the homework please.'
'On the bus, someone took it out of my hand when I was reading it
and threw it away.'
'Really? It better be in tomorrow.'
I turned around to my friends. 'She's so gullible.'
'She sure is,' they told me.

'Excuse now, Child?'
'Oh, er I . . .'
'Well, answer me, Child, don't keep the old waiting too long.'
'Well, I . . .'
'You're taking too long.'
'I, I don . . .'
'Have you got it?'
'No.'
Well, have you got an excuse, Child?'
'No.'

Johanna Laurikainen (11)
Blackheath High School, London

Sister's Vows

I promise we will be friends forever,
In good times and bad we will stay together.

I will never say anything bad about you,
But if I ever did I would make sure you knew.

Any secrets you tell me will not be passed on,
And if you are sad I will never be gone.

If I make new friends I will never leave you out,
My companionship with you should never be in doubt.

If anyone sends a rumour about you or me,
We will stick by each other and show them how strong we can be.

We have a bond that no one can change,
The friendship we have I would never exchange.

If you feel like it is you I am trying to ignore,
Just tell me and I will see you more.

If I leave out your good friend and you think I am wrong,
Don't be afraid to tell me that she does belong.

If I wear something that looks bad,
Telling me it does will make me glad.

Any parties I have you will always come,
I would never let you miss out on the fun.

If you find anything hard,
I will help you whether the problem is small or large.

You are my best friend and I will never leave,
A friend forever is what you should believe.

India Innes (12)
Blackheath High School, London

Angry Paper!

What are you looking at?
Don't hold me too tight!
I know I'm only paper,
But I have feelings, alright?

I used to be plain,
And now I look like this!
Being paper I really miss.

Stop looking at me!
That's enough, okay?
You're being really cheeky,
The fifth today.

Finally,
The writing is almost done
I hope you're happy
And I hope you had fun.

Me? *No!*
Not me, I'm sad
Now I'm angry paper
Because you really made me mad!

Cheyenne Gordon (12)
Blackheath High School, London

Forest Fire

Minute buds of life
Start to spread infectiously
Domino effects

Stretching to the sky
Diabolical fingers
Clawing destiny

Shaking and crackling
Withering in their own heat
Leaping and falling

Catapulting flames
Somersaulting overhead
Diving, cascading

Descending embers
Luminously dancing heat
Drowned of its spirit.

Eleanor Johnston (11)
Blackheath High School, London

Joy

It is bright sunshine-yellow
A room where happiness never ends
Flying free as a bird
Where worries are just a word
Like a tropical island
Uninhabited, hot and sunny
Joy is a big cup full of happiness
Cool tropical juice with a sparkling light
A beautiful sight
Warm and light like a greenhouse
I am a shining star in the sky
Hanging up high
Always smiling
There is nothing to make me cry
I have joy.

Sarah Spicer (12)
Chapter School, Strood

Joy

It is a bright, yellow, warm sunshine,
A room where happiness never ends.
Feeling free, like a bird,
When worries are just a word,
As you travel through the forest of life.

New life giving birth,
Awakening hopes and dreams,
Future promises are unravelling,
Like a bud on a new tree.

Happiness filters through the leaves,
A shimmering light shines upon the seas,
Early morning mist appears,
Bringing with it early morn,
Everything around us seems happy with joy,
As joy is an endless journey that travels through us all.

Aimee Slater (13)
Chapter School, Strood

The Question

I sit and watch the time go by,
I sit and wonder why I died.
Everything was different then,
With the birds and the bees and the little toy men.
Until one day when I found
The most terrible secret ever to be told.
A boy with a gun that dialled 999.
You see it was very simple then.
I ask you, why did I die then?
Did my son have to watch
Or did he join the human rot?
Was it him that killed me
Or someone I beg to differ?
I sit and wonder why
Why did I ever die?

Hollie Hodges
Chapter School, Strood

Best Friends

Best friends, what are they for?

You meet them and you are happy for so long.
Spending time with them, they open a locked door.

They're perfect in every way, and you're long gone.
See them every day and speak on the phone.
Late night sleepover, she's the coolest.

Then it all goes wrong. What happened?
Now I'm alone but really what happened?
She was the best.
I cry each night wondering what I have done.
I don't dare ring, what could I say? What could I do?

Spending my time with her then was so much fun,
Now time goes by, I have nothing to do.
She was the best friend I'd ever had.
I walk alone from now on, very, very sad.

Ellis Bowden
Chapter School, Strood

Love

It always happens more than once
And when it does, gladness
However, when it goes, sadness
Am I good or am I bad?

Whenever I come there is good
When I stay for good, yay!
When I don't come they are lonely
Am I good or am I bad?

I always come to everyone
Be it sooner or later
What am I? Do you know?
I am love!

Ella Mudd (12)
Chapter School, Strood

Who Am I . . . ?

Who am I . . . ?
Sometimes I'm tabby,
But sometimes I'm a tortoise shell.
Who am I? A cat!

Who am I . . . ?
Sometimes I run, sometimes I leap.
I am mostly yellow but have some spots.
Who am I . . . ? A cheetah!

Who am I . . . ?
I swing from tree to tree,
People think I'm cheeky,
I'm very sweet and live in the jungle.
Who am I . . . ? A monkey.

Who am I . . . ?
Sometimes I work,
Sometimes I play,
Sometimes I'm quiet,
But normally I'm noisy.
Who am I . . . ? *Me!*

Nicole Rowlands (11)
Chapter School, Strood

It Hurts

When it happens you see dark blood-red,
also there appears jet-black.
The surroundings are horrible and torture,
there are knives, hammers and it's a feeling that's not good.

This happens when someone dies,
it's a strong, overwhelming feeling,
it leads people to do things they don't want to do,
it's killing, it's pain, does it hurt you?

Michelle McGrath (14)
Chapter School, Strood

Summer Soon Be Gone

It is summer and the tall trees are green,
The wind has settled and the sun is near,
The flowers have grown and bees have been seen,
But there's definitely no need to fear!
It is summer and the days are longer,
So make the most of it and have some fun,
Turn up the volume and join the conga,
Or lay out to get a tan in the sun!

It is summer but it'll soon be gone,
Autumn follows, then winter and then spring,
Fun activities have been going on,
Like us gathered in the garden to sing,
This summer has been lots of fun-filled fun,
With the slight breeze and the glimmering sun!

Siobhan Hards (13)
Chapter School, Strood

Friends

Friends are always there for you,
When you're glad, happy or sad,
And sometimes when you're mad!
A good friend can memorise your mobile and home number
And always knows your ring tone.
They know what to say when things go wrong,
And the phone calls are really long.
They can sort out all your problems and your nerves,
And when your brain is a blurb.
They get on with your family and they play on your trampoline,
And eat your food and your ice cream.

Alexis Maloney (11)
Chapter School, Strood

Gunshot

Lying in bed,
Late at night,
I heard a bang,
It made me jump with fright.

I jumped out of bed,
And crept downstairs,
Pushed open the door,
This is what I saw.

My mother lying in her blood,
It was like an ebony flowing flood,
I tried to scream but nothing came out,
Until I heard my brother's shout.

I turned around,
And fainted quick,
I couldn't stop,
It made me sick.

I was so scared,
I didn't know what to do,
It made me cry,
And my brother too.

I thought of my sister,
Only a tot,
And thought of how I couldn't,
Hear the same horrid gunshot.

Amber Williams (12)
Chapter School, Strood

Guess My Feeling

I feel upset, sad and ready to cry,
My teardrops are falling and all my friends will die,
Screaming and shouting ringing in my ears,
Giving a very high-pitched squeal.

I am falling, falling in a black hole,
I will never stop myself 'cause I'm so alone.

People are laughing and taking the mickey out of me,
Now you know how it feels to be me.
Guess my feeling, you should know!

Sad.

Laura Dyson (12)
Chapter School, Strood

Nobody Knows Me

I'm called this
I'm called that
I don't know if anyone knows me!
I know there's something I should do
I know I should
But nobody knows me.

I'm left here
I'm left there
I'm called 'it' but that's not right!
I'm going to do something
I know I should
But nobody knows me.

What should I do?
I must do it soon
If nobody likes me
I could just ask.

Do you know me?
No!

Elizabeth Fovargue (11)
Chapter School, Strood

Scariness

I shared a room with my sister,
Just last night I kissed her.
I woke up in the middle of the night,
And had such a terrible fright.
The window was open and she had gone,
I screamed but nothing came out.
I got out of bed to tell my mum and dad,
But realised that the curtain was blowing and they had *vanished!*
I just remembered the dream I thought I had!
That voices were talking and footsteps were coming up the stairs.

I went back in my room and realised
That my sister's diary drawer was open.
I was so scared. What should I do?
It's taken my mum, dad and sister. Why didn't it take me?
I'm scared.
I tiptoe downstairs and take a peep in the kitchen.
I see the back door open and a note in the letterbox.
It says, 'I have taken them'.
Help!

Sophie Ruck (12)
Chapter School, Strood

In My Room!

In my room I have . . .
A fluffy blanket, soft and cuddly,
Fluffy cushions as soft as a kitten,
In my warm, cosy bed that is where I rest my head,
Busted playing in my room,
Reminding me of when I went to see them in concert.

In my room I have . . .
Lava lamps, hot and bubbly, just like a bubble bath,
All my teddies to keep me company,
And also my TV so I can watch all the soaps,
I love my room because it's my own.

Aimie Collard (12)
Chapter School, Strood

Joy

It is paradise
Sun, sea, sand
I'm so excited
I feel yellow
I feel bright
Sunshine is all around
My hotel's made of flowers
My bed's so cosy
My pool is so warm
It's like a great, big, lemon, zesty drink
Sour, full of flavour
My mouth waters when I see the ocean
I'm so happy but feel so sad
My parents are nowhere to be found
I feel so lonely but I'm crowded
We've met so many
Lovely people on this great, big, sour, zesty island
So full of flavour, so full of life
I'm so free and so alive!

Georgia-Ann Jeffery & Paris-Ann Wymark
Chapter School, Strood

Emotions

E motions everywhere, some that make you motionless,
M otionless like a sleeping horse,
O r some that make you tired,
T ired and feeling like you're going to collapse.
I gnoring everyone and everything,
O ver the world on cloud nine.
N othing to do but sleep,
S leepiness is what I feel.

Samantha Pugh (12)
Chapter School, Strood

We Add Up To!

Sun and God equals Earth
Here they live on the turf

Mum and Dad equals love
Girl and boy and a flying dove

Bread and butter
Makes us better

Red and pink
Makes us think

We're happy and bright
But sometimes we fight

We're more dangerous than a warhead
But as cute as a teddy in bed

We love to have fun
On our big round bun

We can talk
But sometimes it's like being stabbed with a fork!

We're clever
And we're always together

We are humans!

Nicola Coward (11)
Chapter School, Strood

Joy

Joy is a happy feeling
It shines like the sun
It's as nice as the feeling
Of being loved
It's as nice as a glass of orange juice on a warm day
It's as wonderful as a holiday to France
It's as bright as the colour yellow
Joy is a happy feeling.

Rebecca Steward (12)
Chapter School, Strood

Love

If I could have just one wish,
I would wish to wake up every day
to the sound of your breath on my neck,
the warmth of your lips on my cheek,
the touch of your fingers on my skin,
and the feel of your heart beating with mine . . . .
knowing that I could never find that feeling with anyone other than you.

I love the way you look at me, your eyes so bright and blue.
I love the way you kiss me, your lips so soft and smooth.
I love the way you make me so happy,
and the ways you show you care.
I love the way you say, 'I love you' and the way you're always there.
I love the way you calm me down, always sending chills down my spine.
I love that you are with me, and I am glad that you are mine.

Zoe Beadle (12)
Chapter School, Strood

Cat

I am here on the floor,
Lying down even more,
One stroke, up I jump,
Then I land with a thump.

I am lazy, I am fun,
I am just a little one,
Don't worry, I'm quite small,
Just be careful, I might fall.

I am quick, I am slow,
All you do is let me go,
I eat fast, sleep fast,
Then the day will quickly pass!

Holly Young (12)
Chapter School, Strood

Crazy Clowns

Crazy cows in a field, some are grazing
But others prefer to have a munch
Some would just prefer to sit and gaze
While the rest prefer their lunch

Some of the crazy cows are chocolate-brown
The other crazy cows have patches of black
They love to lounge on the green grass ground
While scratching their soft and curly back

There's always a big, sparkling, blue tear
In those big, gorgeous, huge brown eyes
They never seem to have a fear
As they all just gaze at the big blue skies

I'd just like to say that the best one of all
Is the one on my dinner plate that makes me full.

Jae Lambert
Chapter School, Strood

My Pets!

I have a ferret that is called Poppy,
And I think she is really cute and sweet.
She really loves to be so very hoppy,
On her very tiny, cute, little feet.
I also have an old English bulldog,
Who has a suitable name of Dott.
She has bulgy eyes like a bullfrog,
And has a white coat with a big black spot.
We also have a pet that's called Daisy,
Who is a big, fluffy grey and white cat.
She used to be a little bit crazy,
Until she caught a big brown rat.
These are just a few of our lovely pets,
With all these we are forever at the vet's.

Emma Taylor (13)
Chapter School, Strood

Love

I see him sitting there and I cannot breathe
I wish he would forget about her
I sit and think about them and I heave
I sit and lie on my bed and think and wonder
When he sees me I am just a mate
But when I see him I feel pain
Every day I hope, wish and want a date
The hoping and wanting a date is only just keeping me sane

I wish that he would feel something for me
All I want is for him to look at me differently
Each time I am reminded how great we would be
It feels like I have been kicked in the knee
One day he will love me back, I know
But until then I will be alone.

Daisy Notley
Chapter School, Strood

Treasure

I found a box,
but where was the key?
In sand, in grass or
deep in the sea?

I searched on land,
I searched in sea,
I searched on my own,
but where was the key?

I was falling asleep,
the moon was out,
could the key have legs,
and walk about?

Ellie Chowne (11)
Chapter School, Strood

Isn't It Great When You're In Love?

Isn't it great when you're in love?
Whole lives are bound to change,
Suddenly appears a white dove,
Keep within a close range.

Two people are joined at the hip,
It takes two to be one,
Make sure you don't fall in a dip,
Just make sure you have fun.

Stay together for evermore,
Life is irregular,
Away to the Earth's core,
Love is spectacular.

Never leave each other alone,
You'll never want to part,
Until you start to hear a big drone,
Never mess with your heart.

Can't wait until Valentine's Day
Cupid's little arrow,
You are likely to find a way,
May hit your bone marrow.

Get engaged and then get married,
Have some kids and name them,
Just make sure that you get carried,
Just don't lose your dress hem.

Watch them grow strong and beautiful,
Teach them to respect you,
Together build a waterfall,
They watch Winnie the Pooh.

Have a great family day out,
You can go to the zoo,
You can even get about,
You have a good time too!

Natasha Robinson (13)
Chapter School, Strood

Hitachi

There is a young boy named Hitachi,
Who wanders alone in the park.
Many people ask, 'Who is he?'
The boy who is seen in the dark.

No one has ever seen his face,
Is he Asian, black or white?
He has no shoes to wear on his feet,
Just cloth, leaves and lace.

He carries around in his pocket,
A scroll made of skin.
He wears a small silver locket,
And he is extremely thin.

Has he any family?
No one really knows.
He is just a young and lonely boy,
Who has no friends or foes.

A rumour began to spread around,
That Hitachi was found dead.
In a coffin made of stone,
And this is what it said:

'This town is my home,
It is and will always be,
I'm the happiest boy that ever lived,
Please don't take pity on me.

In my heart I was a man,
But I really was a boy.
I want you all to understand,
That I was full of joy.'

Charlotte McAllen (13)
Chapter School, Strood

Her Love For Him

Her love for him is very strong,
She loves it when he smiles,
He plays all day in the sunshine,
He looks at her with love,
She holds his hand and holds it tight,
He is very precious,
Her love for him will last forever.

Brogan Duke (13)
Chapter School, Strood

Night-Time

Silver moon shining down
Sparkling within the quiet town
Diamond stars, oh so bright
Creating a child's night-time light

Child's special night-time light
Gleaming peacefully through the night
In the fields the night-time grows
The moonlight glitters as the stream flows.

Nicole Arthur (11)
Chapter School, Strood

Into The Sunset

Flowers swaying in a cool summer's breeze,
Children playing with grass on their knees,
Clouds in the sky,
And birds flying high.

The sun starts to set behind the hills,
As two people walk across open fields,
Holding hands, they slowly go,
Into the sunset, it's love that they show,.

Sarah Mahoney (14)
Chapter School, Strood

A Teddy Bear's Promise

I am trying hard,
but I know I can do better,
so I'm writing it down,
to you in this letter.

A promise I will keep,
forever and ever,
for you I will do it,
my sparkling treasure.

My best I will give,
to you every day,
so you will be proud of me,
in each and every way.

Bethany Smith (12)
Chapter School, Strood

My Hamster

My hamster is the best,
He's the one with the furry chest,
He runs up and down at night,
And sleeps when it is light.

One night while we were asleep in bed,
My hamster escaped from his cage and fled,
We searched high and low,
Where did that hamster go?

So we left some food on the floor,
And quietly closed the kitchen door,
And now the best news yet,
We found our favourite pet!
(All soggy and wet!)

Brooke Levick (12)
Chapter School, Strood

Anger

I am a volcano about to blow,
I am the windows shattering,
I am the colour of red,
I am an earthquake rumbling loudly.

I am like an aeroplane crashing,
I am a tornado raging through the forest,
I am a dragon roaring,
I am the hottest part of the flame.

I am the hot sand burning your feet,
I am the angry shark in the rough sea water,
I am the tsunami drowning places,
I am angry!

Lydia Raven (12)
Chapter School, Strood

Lydia Raven

Echolocation

Dolphins have glittering eyes
When they're jumping through the skies
They've always got a smile
But not just a smile, a springy smile.

They have soft, silky skin
With long, luscious fins
Their cries echo with sound
As they swift round, round and round.

They swim through the ocean
With a soft and gentle motion
The sun shines through their skin
Their high-pitched voices sing.

Dollyanna Davies (12)
Chapter School, Strood

Just Boredom

Nothing to do
Bored out of my mind
The cold air hits me
Greyness begins
Like a rock
Dull, nothing to do
A derelict house rotting away
Sits - boredom
The decaying apple orchard
The empty boxes full of nothing
Sit there waiting
For boredom to end.

Hannah Parris (13)
Chapter School, Strood

Untitled

If it were a place it would be a funfair,
full of life, laughter, children and families.
If it were a drink it would be ice-cold Coke,
the cold feel down your throat.
If it were a country it would be America,
alive with music and friendly neighbours.
It's like a yellow hot air balloon,
a beautiful colour with a beautiful view.
It's a bouncy castle, fun for all.
It's a bunny, one person's smile.
Another person smiles for joy.
It's my happiness.

Ursula Byrne
Chapter School, Strood

Brightly

Brightly the stars twinkle in the night sky
Brightly the street lamps shine, making a pathway
Brightly the moon glows, I wonder why
Brightly are the colours from the fireworks as they spark

Brightly the sun shines, radiating a warm glow
Brightly is the laughter of children as they play
Brightly the rain shimmers off the flowing river
Brightly sings the colours we see every day

Brightly the butterfly flies from flower to flower
Brightly the snow lays heavily on the ground
Brightly the rain patters with all its power
Brightly the flowers grow and grow

Brightly the lights glow on the Christmas tree
Brightly the wrapping paper shines on the presents
Brightly our faces glow when we drink a mug of tea
Brightly the fire glows when we eat toasted marshmallows.

Megan Wells (12)
Chapter School, Strood

Boredom On An Island

Nothing to do,
Bored out of my mind,
Stranded on this deserted island.
The only thing for company is the bright moon at night.
The sea as still as a stone.
The only thing to do is look at an old rusty shipwreck.
That smell of a musty old room.
Where is the laughter of my friends?
Where are the neighs of horses?
Where are my family keeping me safe?
Where is my soft, cuddly dog?

Lauren Amy Truelove (13)
Chapter School, Strood

Unrequited

I see you walking on your own,
Quietly, silently, sadly I can see,
I see you there just all alone,
I would so like to find the key . . .

To your heart, I want to unlock it,
I want to find your inner feelings,
I want to unravel them bit by bit,
I want to find your goodness and your sins.

I would like you to feel the same way,
Feel the sadness when you reject me,
Love me the same way that I love you,
Feel the happiness when you care for me.

But I think I like you more in my dreams,
So we'll keep reality just as it seems.

Georgia-May Hales (12)
Chapter School, Strood

Loneliness

Loneliness is the colour of grey
Loneliness is a room of despair
Loneliness is hard to swallow
Loneliness is the smell of nothing
Loneliness is an empty night
All on its own, loneliness is emptiness, nothingness
Altogether, it's sad being on your own.

Hannah Elizabeth Major (13)
Chapter School, Strood

Rainy Day

The rain is coming down, falling on the ground,
Like little crystals just sitting, gleaming,
They fall from the eye of the cloud with no sound,
Just pit-pat, pit-pat like you are dreaming,
You will need your wellies and your raincoat,
There is no sun today, just wish the rain away,
If it lasts all day, we will need a boat,
There's a little sun now, making the rainbow today,
Knock, knock, everyone is in hiding,
They fear the clouds and his crystal drops,
The song of the wind is also guiding,
But people aren't happy, just wait till it stops,
It has stopped now but the clouds are still there,
Please don't start again, please don't dare.

Kirsty Mayle
Chapter School, Strood

Stressed Out

I feel like a jet speeding,
A balloon popping.

A lion running for food but not successfully,
A volcano ready to explode.

A fire burning and spitting,
An engine blowing.

A hurricane rushing around,
An earthquake shaking the world.

But nothing could stop the anger from growing.

Rebecca Anne Bell (11)
Chapter School, Strood

The Elderly!

Some people tend to forget the old,
Surely the elderly believe that is so,
We mustn't forget they're precious like white gold,
We have to appreciate how much they know,
Often they're treated as though they were babies,
When we put them in homes, we don't realise,
That maybe they have feelings too, so just maybe,
They're not old through someone else's eyes,
In nursing homes they may feel neglected,
Being old surely should not be a crime,
Society makes them feel rejected,
But they know we'll all become old in time,
As we treat the old, so may we be treated
We all know history tends to be repeated!

Emily Still (13)
Chapter School, Strood

Arrow Of Love

There's a spark off a candle that lights us with bloom,
Love takes its time to find, it feels so slow,
Love is an arrow, that we assume,
Cupid's the one that fires it so,
A shiny arrow leaping across the sky,
Two people thinking of each other,
A lovely sweet dinner like chicken pie,
Precious love is from a father and mother,
Roses are red, the colour of our heart,
That can be easily broken by silly mistakes,
Nothing will keep the love apart,
That's soft and gentle like a snowflake,
The flight of the heart, the landing of the dove,
Reaching out for the one you love.

Katy Lowe (13)
Chapter School, Strood

Gravity

Gravity, what a pain in the neck
I'm really quite confused
What is it? Why is it?
And who should we accuse?

Oh, Isaac Newton, that was who
What a clever man
An apple fell and hit the ground
And Isaac Newton ran.

He leapt in the air and fell back down
He wondered how it worked
He stopped, stood still and thought awhile
This made him more alert.

Then he rang his friend I think
From the planet Mars
He said he stays up in the air
And can almost touch the stars.

This proves that gravity only exists
On this planet here
I think Sir Isaac Newton
Deserves a great big cheer.

Hooray!

Charlotte Shuter (13)
Charters School, Sunningdale

Vacuum Of Life

In my heart there is a vacuum,
Yet no room for anything inside,
In my head there is emptiness,
Yet no space for any thoughts,
In my eyes, sharp needles stab,
Under my hand, sand runs like a river,
Beneath my feet lie my hopes and dreams.

Carey Leedham (15)
Charters School, Sunningdale

Gravity

Flying, like a bird, no gravity,
Flying high, with no care at all,
But if you really were flying high,
Then it would end with a painful fall.

Floating with the moon and the stars,
Floating through the mystical sky,
But if that did well and truly happen,
You would hit the floor and could die.

The sky, so dark and magical,
As you glide into the black,
But in the world, in true reality,
You could fall and break your back.

So next time you dream of flying,
Flying across the very still sea,
Remember it's dangerous and unlikely,
Due to the strength of gravity.

Bertie Galliford (13)
Charters School, Sunningdale

Forecast

Drips tap at the panes.
The window is crying again.
Water wells from the frame
Seeping down the glass to line
Tears on her reflection.
A crystal clear
Complexion.

Alone outside, the wind whimpers.
But understands
Far too late
This time.

Joseph Hedinger (16)
Charters School, Sunningdale

Gravity

Gravity, the nails in our feet that keep us down,
Holding the king to his crown,
The powerful depiction of a parallel universe,
Like a belt to keep us from being able to disperse.

Making the force of nature uphold its balance,
And with these magical talents,
It makes nature keep up with its own survival,
But what kind of power can hold this title?

Gravity - that heavy sensation,
The very strain on life's exploration,
Yet the key to life's creation,
Living through every dimension.

The eternal element that comes without explanation,
But with a lot of deep contemplation,
From an apple to its core,
From space to the floor.
This is one very special case,
But what is this element we face?

Gravity of course,
And as we fall victim to no remorse,
It will occasionally crush and destroy,
As it has death and pain to deploy.

Yet what plagues us with this will to explore?
Is it the way a feather falls to the floor?
Is it how much we weigh
Or is it more to do with what scientists say?

Picture it as a miracle,
Like an endless trilogy or chronicle,
Like an invisible force,
That which is the force of love.

A stairway to answers,
A place of glowing dancers,
A place only in dreams,
At least that's what it seems.

The leap for humanity,
The stairway to insanity,
Yes, it's gravity.

Hassanin Yousif (15)
Charters School, Sunningdale

Gravity

There's an invisible force of which we're not aware,
It's really simple so don't despair.
Hold a ball and feel the weight,
It's very simple, and a normal state.

The force that acts, the force that pulls,
The downward force is gravity.
The apple that fell on Newton's head,
Was the invisible pull of gravity.

Without it you would float away,
The force of it acts every day.
It controls the planets and the stars,
And stops us coming to undue harm.

The unseen force,
Which controls our lives,
Allowing us to duck and dive.
Where would we be without the force of gravity?

Emily Graham (13)
Charters School, Sunningdale

Gravity

A man falls to his feet,
Weak to the power of nicotine,
He takes 20 a day,
Plenty a night.

Gravity.

Not aware of the power,
Not aware of the consequence,
Not aware of the money,
A blind man lost in thoughts and addiction.

Gravity.

He lies in bed,
Not able to move,
His breathing short,
A lot to lose.

Gravity.

A trip to hospital,
Bad news to arrive,
No one to help,
No one to hear.

Gravity.

Illness surging through his veins,
Playing with his mind,
Dancing with his lungs,
Digging his own grave.

Gravity!

Jasmine Hughes (13)
Charters School, Sunningdale

Marvin On Gravity!

Life, don't talk to me about life
my left diodes need changing and my head's too big
I'm a man made of metal
and it isn't getting any better

A brain the size of a planet
it's positively depressing
I can do nearly any calculation
and what do they ask me to do?

To talk to a room full of morons
about the simplest thing
that thing that keeps you
down on the ground, gravity.

The people of Gregrundy,
can fly in the air
because they're so stupid
and just don't believe

whereas the three-headed dogs of Wooflington
can barely lift a limb
by naming their god after this force
it gained so much to conquer within.

So my conclusion today
is that you have no brains
and I am terribly depressed
but please listen when I say,

gravity will squash you flat!

Abi Trainor (13)
Charters School, Sunningdale

Where Would We Be Without Gravity?

As we look towards the luminous sky
We ask, question, wonder why
Where would we be? Where would we go?
What would happen if it were so?
But I answer with a simple conundrum
If it would go, and instead have none
We may soar through the hot summer sky
And be like birds with the ability to fly
We rise up above without a worry or care
As the ground as we know it has been lifted to air
We glide with our pets, our family, our friends
How we flip, swirl, roll and bend,
Until one day we realise instead
That to stop other than go ahead
Is actually, in fact, out of our reach
We can't cry *help!* or even preach
As we continue to yell, we continue to rise
Up and up, placed freely in the skies
But without the restrictions, we haven't a clue
As where to go or as what to do
We continue to rise and travel so high
Awaiting the inevitable, of course, to die
You see without would be a terrible mistake
As the world as we know it would unleash its fate
So this is the rhetorical question I ask at the end
Where would we be without gravity?

Nicola Crane (13)
Charters School, Sunningdale

Gravity

Bang!
With the fire of a pistol,
Into his head,
A quick death
But why?
He didn't mean to do it!
It just happened.
He never meant to get angry!
It just happened.
He didn't mean to pull the trigger!
It just happened.
But that was it.
The end of his son.
His corpse lay on the floor
Blood oozing from his head.
The floor was painted red
With his son's blood,
His blood.
The gravity of the situation
Hit him
Hit him hard
And he fell.
There he was
Bathing in his son's blood.
He never meant for it to happen
It just happened.

Joe Conlan (13)
Charters School, Sunningdale

Gravity Situation

A scream rings around the house,
It's heard from down the street.
Everyone in the house
Is alerted to their feet.

'What's happened? What's happened?
What has gone wrong?'
The scream still echoes,
The birds stop their song.

'This is serious, real serious!'
A voice cries out.
Everyone rushes to see,
This must be terrible without a doubt.

'This is seriously, seriously bad!
One hundred percent disaster!
Totally, utterly, stupidly serious!'
Heart rates speed up and go faster.

'So you're not joking then.'
'Of course I'm not!
It's serious, factor one hundred and ten!'
The baby stands up in its cot.

'I've lost my slippers! What a disaster,
I cannot live without them!'
'That's not bad, I thought you were dying!
Do you know you're wearing them?'

Andy MacIntyre (13)
Charters School, Sunningdale

Homeless

I should never have left home,
Living on the streets is awful and I feel so alone,
Trying to find somewhere to sleep; a floor made of tile, brick or stone,
The floor is hard, I feel cramped and chilled to the bone.

Now I'm settled for the night,
In my sleeping bag, snuggled up nice and tight,
Then along comes a bloke, twice my height,
Says, 'Give me your money or do you want to fight?'

So, I'm lying awake . . .
Along come some louts who I absolutely hate,
Thank God they don't see me . . . it must be getting late,
So I lie listening for footsteps, voices and breathing, it's a very
long wait.

I can't get to sleep,
So cold are my feet,
It's so quiet, I can hear my heart beat,
All I want now is a bit of heat.

Oh, what I would give for a slice of bread,
Or my soft, comfy, four-poster bed,
If I don't eat soon I will be dead,
That's what all the other homeless children said.

I'm so despaired,
Nothing, no one ever cared,
About me, nobody dared,
I feel so homesick and so scared.

Living on the streets is awful and I feel so alone,
Oh I wish, I wish I had never left home.

Sofia von Sachsen-Altenburg (14)
Charters School, Sunningdale

Help Them Now!

People are dying every day, every hour,
Every minute and every second.
Poverty spreads like a flowing river.
Disease thriving,
Illness ruling the entire community, entire country.
Do people really understand the gravity of this situation?
People die with no one beside them.
Children orphaned by an awful disease.
Will anyone help?
Will anyone give?
Will anyone support?
Children forever walking along streets with nowhere to go.
There is no hygiene, no health, no help
And that is the way it shall always be.
Unless we help.
Do you understand the gravity of this situation?

Vicky Lonsdale (13)
Charters School, Sunningdale

Gravity

It's like elastic superglued to your struggling feet,
As soon as you leave the ground,
You come speeding back,
It roams the Earth,
Locking your feet in a ball and chain,
Keep wondering what it is like to soar through the air,
Gliding with great power through the soft, pearly clouds,
But instead we're stuck on this hard, cold ball of crust,
Gravity.

Rebecca Tregoiing (12)
Charters School, Sunningdale

Pain

Alone in the darkness,
She cries and cries,
Each minute aching more than the last,
She wishes it was over, over . . .
. . . Time dwells as she takes the next,
To finish her endless pain,
A life so small, yet so big,
Heart filled with sorrow,
She cries and cries,
She takes another pill,
She loses her will,
Horrendous pain through her frail, thin body,
Lifeless and drained,
Anger inside, wants to die, losing her mind,
The tears fall, trickling down her scar-ridden face,
Bitter resentment to life,
She closes her eyes, she becomes a lonely soul . . .
. . . She pops another,
Her hurt is soothed, she cannot move,
She cries and cries,
It's over.

Laura Clarke (13)
Charters School, Sunningdale

The Poem With No Name

It pins down emotions,
It takes away happiness,
It has no choice,

It follows pain and suffering,
It follows anger and defeat,
It has no choice,

It causes chaos, little and big,
It shocks and awes,
It is sorry,

It has its friends,
They wander wherever they please,
It is sorry,

If we didn't have it we'd be lost,
Lost to all oblivion,
Most of the time it's alone,

Rain.

Harriet Crofton (13)
Charters School, Sunningdale

Gravity - Seriousness

Am I worth anything at all?
Why do they mock me at my school?
Does anyone care about what I say?
I don't see what's wrong with me anyway?
Am I different to the others?
I thought we all were meant to be brothers.
They do fine, they get along,
I don't see what we've all done wrong.
Why do the fingers all point at me?
Why won't they let me be?
The teachers know but they don't care,
I still don't know why all the kids stare.
Their words make me feel very bad,
But they smile and laugh, then walk away glad.
Sometimes their comments make me shudder,
All of this caused by my skin colour.
I do not mock them as they are white,
But in the future other black people might.
In the future the tables might turn,
Then my people's comments will scratch and burn.
Soon enough my people will fight back,
Then it will be cool to be a black.
But I can't see why we can't all get along,
Live in unity and do no wrong.

Harry Rudman (12)
Charters School, Sunningdale

Gravity Poem

Night sings gently,
In your dreams.
Desires are truths,
In your head.

Sultry youth surrounds you,
While happiness bounds you.
This is the land of imagination,
This is the land of make-believe.

Danger no longer exists,
Work is no longer done.
Dreams become reality,
Never wishing to return.

But the harsh truth hits you,
As you awake from your slumber.
Life is no longer a fairy tale,
The gravity of time returns.

In corners of your mind,
Demons softly taunt you.
And hidden in the shadows,
They swiftly follow you.

Despair and boredom engulf you,
As you work hard through the day.
Upset and failure rule you,
As you slowly trudge home alone.

The seriousness is lifted,
As you gently settle into bed.
The demons slowly dissolve,
And dreams surface instead.

Enjoy the rest from daylight,
Make the most of lies.
Let your imagination run riot,
Enjoy the land of make-believe . . .

Megan Harrington (13)
Charters School, Sunningdale

Gravity

There she was, smiling happily,
Having lots of fun.
But behind the smile hides a secret,
Worse than any other.
Never to be told, as the fear and the dismay,
Looms over her abandoned heart.
Puzzled and scared.
Worried and threatened.
Panic-stricken,
Wishing it would all end.
That never again would she have
To live with the pain.
No more haunting nightmares of her terror.
The gravity of this situation is so enclosed,
That nobody will ever know.

Katie Mathews (13)
Charters School, Sunningdale

Gravity

Newton discovered gravity,
When he saw the apple fall.
If there was no gravity,
We would float across the hall.
Newton said that gravity,
Came from under our feet,
But, without gravity,
We will be off our seat.
You can't live without gravity,
Because everything would be in the air.
It would be very hard,
Trying to sit on a chair.
Some people thought that he was brainless,
But without gravity, we would be weightless!

Zahra Rajabalipour (13)
Charters School, Sunningdale

Gravity

I will drag you down,
pull you down
like a bout of depression.
Even if your spirits soar
and your feet begin to leave
the ground in exaltation
I can drag you back to earth.

I was not discovered for any reason,
now I'm here I'll stay,
even if rockets can combat my force,
I am a force and I will keep the balance.
I threw the apple
realise my strength.

I am stronger than all humans,
I am a law in physics,
a law,
a rule,
made not to be broken.

I will drag you down,
pull you down,
down . . .
down.

Melanie Todd (16)
Charters School, Sunningdale

Gravity

Why can't I reach the stars?
Why can't I jump to Mars?
For space is far away,
I stay at Earth and play.

If I jump,
It pulls me down,
For life,
I'm stuck on the ground.

It has a science name,
It plays a part in netball games,
If it had no effect on me,
I'd be as wild as a bumble bee.

For it guides our way,
It is here every day,
Gravity keeps me down.

Emily Finnemore (13)
Charters School, Sunningdale

Gravity

Battling with the misty sky,
Wind whipping through my hair.
Up, up, up I go,

As if I were climbing a ladder.
No, wait, I'm floating on the clouds,
Looking down on loyal citizens.

My toes brush past the treetops,
Up, up, up I go.
I look down, I see little specs of dirt,

Higher and higher I climb.
Defining gravity,
For now, it's enough to know.
Apples fall and carelessly bruise,

The sea is gleaming below.
A boat afloat would come and go,
Up, up, up I go!

Kerry Deans (13)
Charters School, Sunningdale

Gravity Bringing Me Down

Lose yourself in a daydream,
Get lost deep in thought.
Float away to a distant world,
Where wishes become reality.

Fly with ease in a moonlit sky,
Or see the wonders of the deep blue sea.
In a place where anything is possible,
You can live a life free from harm.

But watch out while you are living it up,
And brushing the dawn-lit clouds.
Because this land doesn't last forever,
And neither does make believe.

Without any warning at all,
You can be snatched back to the real world.
Brought down by the demons of gravity,
Taking you back to the serious reality.

The thought of evil and worry comes back,
Dark whispers disturb your distant world.
You fall in deep black despair,
Bringing you down, down, down . . .

Hayden Stagg (13)
Charters School, Sunningdale

Shahrazad

My feet carry the sores and blisters,
of a thousand and one journeys.
Bearing my load.
We are those left behind;
forgotten, whilst our men flew away on wild escapades,
to enjoy caves of golden delicious treasure,
winking lavender princesses.
Our eyes are only full of dust and tears.

Still we dream
of a whole new world
where adventures are more than stories
and carpets fly instead of being cleaned.
Somewhere where no one can tell us no, where to go.
Where Aladdin is free and single
and genies always give four wishes.

Jason Keen (16)
Charters School, Sunningdale

Situation

Nothing.
Just nothing.
I've lost it all.
My money, my family, my life.
For in my darkest days I was always dead.
A living corpse, a shadow of a god.
But now . . .
Nothing.
I let darkness into my heart.
The piercing knife of the Devil tore it apart.
The spectres drank it up and grew.
For now I know the gravity of the situation.
I've brought the world to its knees.
I can't go on, I can't.
When will this nightmare end?
Never. Because I'm nothing.

William Alexander (13)
Charters School, Sunningdale

Gravity

There is a certain button,
That if you press,
It would turn on gravity with a tick,
What would happen if there was no button?

If it wasn't for gravity,
The buildings of the Earth would be bobbing up and down in the sky.
If it wasn't for gravity,
Your bed would be a soft white cloud.

If it wasn't for gravity,
You would play football in mid-air.
If it wasn't for gravity,
Cars would float around in the sky.

But because of gravity's force,
We have buildings on land.
We play football on the pitch,
And all in all our beds stay firmly on the ground.

Faaizah Ikram (13)
Charters School, Sunningdale

Gravity

Gravity,
Soaring me high like a bird,
Dropping me low like an eagle swooping down to catch its prey,
The grass swinging beneath my toes,
Attached firmly to the crumbling chocolate soil,
Air being sucked out of the Earth,
Falling, falling . . .
Energy, life, humans gone,
A bare land,
Objects flying,
The end is simple . . . no gravity.

Rhianne Blockley (12)
Charters School, Sunningdale

Gravity

Gravity is the light of my life!
It makes me sit and stand.
Gravity is there,
It helps me keep aware,
For it is the light of my life.

It helps me see my best friends,
It helps our friendship never end!

But imagine, imagine . . .

The world up high,
Deep in the sky.
No space for cars or trucks,
No men to dig up things,
Not diamonds, not rings,
That world with no gravity!

Our world has gravity,
England, Ireland and Wales,
The Earth!

Lily Robinson (12)
Charters School, Sunningdale

Gravity

It's such a moving force
as it pulls you down unseen
but if it wasn't there
where might we have been?

We may be on the moon
or swimming in the stars
or floating along on our backs
past Jupiter or Mars.

But think what we may do
if that force, it wasn't there
all the girls and long-haired boys
would have floaty, wavy hair.

But the consequences would be dire
they would burn us like a fire
what would happen to all the lakes?
And how would we flip pancakes?

Saul Jones (13)
Charters School, Sunningdale

Dragonfly Blues - Haiku

A dragonfly sat
On a lilypad, her wings
Lapis in the sun.

Fern Coleman (12)
Farlington School, Horsham

Washed Away

Click, click
Knit one, purl one
Click, click
Knit one, purl one
Television blaring
Switch off the news
Patter, patter
Drip, drip
Click, click
Knit one, drip
Click, click
Patter, patter
Swoosh, whoosh
Drummer, drummer
Have you heard the drummer?
He's playing on the rooftops
Brr, brrrr
Shut the windows
A storm's coming
Mark my words
Water, water
Seeping through the door
Up the stairs
Faster, faster
Water's rising
Flooding the floor
Level with the first step
The second
The third
The stairs are underwater
Climbing up my legs
Water, water everywhere
Swim for the steeple,
Frantic strokes
And then -
Nothing.

Lucy Wild (12)
Farlington School, Horsham

Last Dance

The lights dim,
The curtain rises;
Hush falls,
The theatre's silent.
The violins play,
The ballet begins.

The crowd gasped
The moment was mine.
I leapt up high,
Flew across the stage;
I danced the show
With beauty and grace.

The memories of my glory,
The life gone by;
That flame in me
Will never die.
The dance I loved;
My joy.

Others seek to follow
In my steps;
I am confined
To sit and rest.
My body is old
But my mind dances on.

Alex Dockreay (14)
Farlington School, Horsham

Dancing Bananas

At night when the house lies still in its rest,
The bananas come out and do what they do best,
They flip, they dangle and swing from the ceiling,
They really are extremely appealing!
The bananas then leap off the kitchen table,
They really are most amazingly able
And you and I, and no one can guess,
That dancing is what the bananas do best!

They leap off the side and land on their bellies,
They bounce and hop on the strawberry jellies!
They play and then start to fight with bread sticks,
They flip and somersault and show off their tricks!
And you and I, and no one can guess,
That dancing is what the bananas do best!

They pick up an orange and begin to bowl,
And the orange then starts to roll and roll.
The bananas dance and party and bop,
They laugh and they giggle, they run and they hop.
They fill up the sink, and dive right in,
They jump off the edge and land on top of the bin.
And you and I, and no one can guess,
That dancing is what the bananas do best!

Then in the morning, when the cockerel crows,
When the children are putting on their school clothes.
The bananas then start to fall straight to sleep,
In their fruit bowl, in an enormous heap.
And you and I, and no one can guess,
That dancing is what the bananas do best!

Rosie Glasse (13)
Farlington School, Horsham

These I Have Loved

These I have loved;
Crisp new-fallen snow, untouched; hugs; butterflies in the sunlight;
the plop of a tennis ball on summer days; home;
swishing silk; my teddy bear upon my bed;
mountains; cold gurgling streams; sun on a summer morning;
newly-cleaned silver, glimmering; memories; glistening raindrops;
the colours of autumn; family; snow resting on trees;
horse's snort on a misty morning; icicles shining;
lightning etched into a dark sky; hot buttered toast;
flickering flames; smooth, washed stones; layers of soft, white cloud;
freshly cut grass; friends; waves lapping the shore;
lambs frolicking in spring; hot chocolate with cream;
raindrops on roses; a bird's sweet song;
mountain peaks above clouds; smell of Sunday roast; bed;
laughter; trickling water; newly waxed skis; rustle of a duvet;
a dog's wet nose; crisp, cold of a winter morning;
smooth sea; mountain peaks in a sunset; splash of water;
cloudless sky; bird's soft feathers; deep valleys;
the smile of loved ones; cool breeze;
water; glossy hair; hope; cat's fur; trust;
relief from pain; iced drink on a hot day;
warmth; an owl's soft call; a star-scattered sky;
smoke from a chimney; love;
a gap in the clouds where the sun beams through;
the noise of a wet trampoline; spring daffodils; newly-washed clothes;
delicate snowflakes; the clop of hooves on cobbles; glossy chestnuts;
jewels twinkling; serenity.
All of these have been my loves!

Ella Slater (13)
Farlington School, Horsham

These I Have Loved . . .

These I have loved . . .
A blazing log fire on a snow-scattered day;
The scent of fresh bread baking in the oven;
Teddy bears and animals, all things cute;
A red rose drenched in dew;
Sunrise and sunset, a clear, starry night;
Leaping dolphins; the bark of a dog;
Hugs and kisses; laughter and smiles;
My bed; my house; my family all around;
A new car's scent; the taste of foreign cuisine;
Waking up and realising it's Saturday;
Reading a good book; spending time with friends;
Opening my wallet to find money;
Music on a rainy day;
The feeling of relief when a test or project is over;
My daft dogs, bounding around a field;
Fridays; holidays; summer and winter;
The taste of my parents' cooking; chocolate;
All these have been my loves.

Olivia Easton (13)
Farlington School, Horsham

A Seasonal Poem

Spring
When farmers come out to put out new bedding,
It is clear to them now that spring is now spreading.
Sheep in the fields of pastures of green,
If you're not careful wolves can be seen.

Summer
The warmth of the sun on hot summer days,
As the waves roll in on numerous bays.
Let's take a chance and go camping in France,
Everyone around is joining in the dance.

Autumn
Blankets of leaves lay on the ground,
If you look closely, conkers can be found.
When the hedgehogs are asleep and all is well,
That is when the fairies come; what news have they to tell?

Winter
Hot chocolate and cream in a great big cup,
Mum walks through the door with an abandoned pup.
You hide in your homes afraid of Jack Frost,
He blows his cold winter over Dad's compost.

Catriona Dunlop (13)
Farlington School, Horsham

The Tiger

Not a sound - not the crack of a twig,
As the tiger stalks his prey,
His belly glued to the rustling leaves,
His mind never wand'ring away.

He creeps along, every muscle poised,
But tail held jauntily high.
One wrong move could be fatal, he knows,
And he'll end up as 'tiger pie'.

Through the jungle he slowly prowls,
Wide eyes and waggling ears.
He's ever alert and ready to act,
If any small sound he hears.

Then he stops; stock-still and tense,
But his tail swishes to and fro.
In a blink he drops to the ground.
He has no further to go.

Into the open, he springs on his prey,
It has no time to cry out.
Claws sink in, he's won; it's dead.
He gives his victory shout.

Now that it's over he pads to his den -
His family won't starve today.
The lawn is quiet, his prey doesn't move,
'Til wind blows the leaf away.

The kitten's asleep on his rug by the fire.
He'll learn to hunt - another day.

Bethany Jones (13)
Farlington School, Horsham

Walking Through The Woods On A Day In April

Walking through the woods on a day in April,
Watching dismal, grey clouds like puffs of smoke
Drift slowly across the sky,
Aware of a misty curtain of rain coating everything
In a thin sheet of water,
I gaze over the landscape,
Taking in every detail of Mother Nature:

Trees, covered in different shades of green,
Some old, some new, trees that watch
Everything go by, from the changing seasons to
The passing wildlife.
Dead leaves scattered on the ground,
Each a different hue; some a burning orange, others
A chocolate brown.
Broken branches and twigs lying between rows
Upon rows of daffodils and a carpet of newly-grown bluebells,
Their long, thin appearance, like that of a snake.
Birds chirping cheerful tunes.
Rabbits leaping with their strong hind legs and nibbling
Contentedly on luscious grass,
And placid pools of water, created by those famous
April showers.

Walking through the woods on a day in April,
A great feeling of joy erupts inside me as I think to myself,
Lucky are those who can see nature at its best.

Rebecca Ayling (14)
Farlington School, Horsham

Sadness

Sadness is like a dagger stuck right through your heart,
It is like you're in jail and they've thrown away the key,
It is like an ever-onward shadow, never letting you see the light,
It is like a big herd of elephants ready to stamp on you,
Not leaving a piece,
It is like you are stuck to rot in a dark room,
But when you feel sadness it won't leave you alone!

Jasmine Francus (11)
Farlington School, Horsham

Tears

Fall,
Fall softly,
Just like rain.
Wet, salty drops,
Falling on my face,
Running over my cheeks,
Dropping close to my nose.
Hair hiding me from the world,
Hand over my eyes, shielding them,
Shielding trickling tears, shielding me.
My body shaking silently from my misery,
Lips clamped tightly shut like a trapdoor,
Keeping me silent, keeping the tears in.
My misery engulfs me like a black cloud,
I am stuck within, never to be freed,
Sitting here alone, so, so alone,
Me and my tears.

Felicity Jones (15)
Farlington School, Horsham

Lions And Monsters

Many nail-bitten months had passed and still no word,
She sat rigid in the chair by the dying fire,
No company, no children had she, no little ones to tuck up,
And to tell terrifying stories of lions and monsters,
So there she sat every night till sleep's heavy blanket
Weighed her down.

Boom! Enemy shellfire filled every fibre of his strained body,
Deaf to the machine guns that drilled in his skull,
Scared to shut his eyes and have the rats eat his fingers.
But what many a doomed man had told him,
'Keep digging, dig until your body screams at you to stop.'
'Keep firing, fire even when all your friends are dead
And you stand alone.'
'A true man would rather keep his honour than his life,' they spat.

Out to collect the morning milk, she heard a noise from next door,
Old Marge, poor girl, her husband's dead,
Another notch in Germany's sword.
She saw a man in uniform proceed on down the road,
'Wait!' she cried, her heart beating fast as she ran out in the rain.
'Alan, Alan Bradford, any news of him?' she asked the man in grey,
The officer frowned and looked at his list,
Which contained many a name,
He lifted his face slowly to hers, a face that bore no sorrow,
'Alive, Mam,' he said, 'alive and well, he'll be back sometime
tomorrow.'

Hannah Brodrick (15)
Farlington School, Horsham

Untitled

(Inspired by 'Undertones of the War')

On Monday morning,
'Only a boy - only a boy'
Murmured the Scotsman
As he shed tears
Never to be seen again, only tarnished memories
Replaying in my mind
Light does not gleam upon the immediately following
Journey
However dimly in my notions
From another long column
To another long column
Savage! Revolt! Emotion! No defence!
Machine guns there thudded at their targets
Blood
Masked
Bodies
Dead and alive
Evil quickness, no defence, gaping wounds
Dark tunnels, voices crying out, but nothing could be heard,
Except the jerking of the rifle
Grenade delusions playing in my mind
Through the dark trench
Rumbling wheels
That sinister war was not far off!
Making the world safe, for democracy.

Joy Mpofu (15)
Farlington School, Horsham

The Magic Box

(Based on 'Magic Box' by Kit Wright)

I will put in the box . . .

a stunning sunset sinking into the sea,
the pot of gold from an Irish leprechaun,
the answer to the question, 'What is the reason for war?'

I will put in the box . . .

a marble statue's beating heart,
the smell of morning
and golden rain from a silver cloud.

I will put in the box . . .

an indigo secret belonging to a friend
the last present left on Christmas Day
and the first flight of a baby bird.

I will put in the box . . .

a thirteenth hour and a blue moon,
an angel in Hell
and a devil at the gates of Heaven.

My box is fashioned from jewels, rainbows and crystal,
with stories in the corners and the moon, stars and sun on the lid,
with sapphire forget-me-knots entwined around the clasp.

I shall ride through my box
through the rusty autumn woods of England,
then soar up into a cloudless blue sky
and float on the feathers of a dozen white swans.

Olivia Barclay-Hudson (13)
Farlington School, Horsham

My Magic Box

(Based on 'Magic Box' my Kit Wright)

I will put in my box . . .
    The beat of a horse's gallop over the ghostly moor,
    The growl of a dogfish as it swims between the reeds,
    And the wave that runs forever over the crystal sea.

I will put in my box . . .
    The touch of a warm snowflake,
    Upon a solid black cloud,
    And the answer to the question, 'What does war achieve?'

I will put in my box . . .
    The love and peace that should be in this world,
    The first glimpse of a mountain's summit,
    And the last gunshot of a pointless war.

I will put in my box . . .
    A black star and a colourless rainbow,
    An angel with no halo,
    And a devil with no fire.

My box is fashioned from the deepest of pure water,
Dancing tropical fish line the lid of my box,
In the corners are forgotten myths,
And my box is lined with emerald moss.

My box will set free . . .
    The captured animals walking round and round in slow circles,
    Lost in their minds, enclosed behind bars,
    And the horrors left in the minds of soldiers.

Matilda Sims (13)
Farlington School, Horsham

The Blind Man

A blind man walks through his garden,
And touches with sensitive fingers:
The velvet petal,
The piercing thorn,
Of the roses that border his soft springy lawn.

A blind man walks through his garden,
And hears with keen ears:
The crickets on cello,
The bullfrogs sing bass,
As nature's orchestra sets life's easy pace.

A blind man walks through his garden,
And smells with perceptive nose:
The lavender's sweet scent,
The fresh fragrance of grass,
As outside, perfumes blowing on the wind pass.

A blind man walks through his garden,
And tastes with receptive tongue:
The sweet tip of a strawberry,
The salt on the breeze,
As the sand blows over from nearby seas.

A blind man walks through his garden,
And comes to the end by the wall:
Last summer he saw there were five trees,
Now his hands tell him there are four,
But those that remain are still beautiful, and stronger than before.

Katherine Hawkes (11)
Farlington School, Horsham

My Hero

A hero is somebody,
a hero is anybody,
a hero is special,
in many different ways.

I could be a hero,
you could be a hero,
she could be a hero,
he could be a hero.

A hero could save the world,
a hero could do great things,
but that's not my hero,
my hero does other things.

My hero pulls on her gloves,
and does the washing up,
my hero does the ironing,
and travels miles to pick me up.

She loves and cares for me,
unlike any other would,
my hero is *my mum* of course,
important, kind and good.

Rebecca Wycliffe (13)
Farlington School, Horsham

World

We needed some heroes,
So they came,
With their tanks and guns,
And then we found,
We really didn't need them.

We needed medical help,
So they came,
With their plagues and diseases of their own,
And then we found,
We really didn't need them.

Then we needed more help,
But were afraid to ask,
They might come and ruin us again,
And we might find,
That we really don't need them.

Now we are all dying,
And the world just stands and stares,
No help for us, who asked too late,
Who waited too long to see,
That only in dying are we finally free.

Hayley Davies (14)
Farlington School, Horsham

Devastation And Destruction

As the immense wall of water reaches the edge of the beach,
People begin to run for cover.
A brave woman darts towards the wave,
She shouts a warning as it engulfs the land.

As the muddy water surges through the streets,
Utter devastation.
A building collapses like a tower of foam.
People's possessions are swept away,
Like their lives,
Forever lost.

As the wave advances,
Trees fall like dominoes,
The noise shattering the calm,
As they fall slowly into the hastening water.

The frenzied water begins to calm,
Debris and destruction,
The orphaned and the homeless,
Forlorn.
Rebuilding their lives,
But not alone.

Georgia Page (13)
Farlington School, Horsham

These I Have Loved

These I have loved:
Crisp morning light flooding through half-open curtains;
The scrumptious aroma of home baking; family;
The soft touch of newly laundered sheets; friendly faces;
The warm embrace from those who are dear;
The cosy warmth of a roaring log fire; laughter and smiles.

The fresh fragrance of newly-cut grass; spring's lambs;
A carpet of bluebells in a shady wood; snowflakes;
The quick flash of a kingfisher under a bridge;
Dewdrops glistening on rose petals; dragonflies;
And a shaft of light through a leafy glade.

The mystical crescent moon; a starry night;
Skies which are sapphire, candyfloss clouds and birds in flight;
Stripped trees silhouetted against industrial buildings;
Waters ripple; and lavender in cottage gardens.
All of these have been my loves.

Charlotte Hawkes (14)
Farlington School, Horsham

My Soldier

I lie in bed feeling alone,
Wondering if you will ever come home,

I hear the voices in my head,
I can still hear the words that you said,

You left me here in distress,
Acting as if you couldn't care less,

I know you love me deep inside,
So why do you have to run and hide?

You went on your mission only saying goodbye,
But the way you said it just made me cry,

You said you hated me, I knew you were lying,
You closed the door and left me crying,

The moonlight shone into my darkened room,
I hoped that you would come home soon,

Then that night the news finally came,
And then I knew it would never be the same,

I'm lying in bed feeling so alone
Knowing that you will never come home.

Emma Fleming (13)
Hampton Community College, Hampton

In My World

In my world
Unicorns leap over rainbows,
The blue glittering fresh rivers flow.
In my world I feel at peace,
I'm always at ease,
To see the valleys full of flowers,
And eagles soaring over mountains,
Makes me feel like I have powers,
I watch the falling curtains of water fountains,
I stare at my reflection in the rivers,
And snap out of my world with the shivers,
To know that it's not real makes me feel
Sad, insecure and worried;
Instead we all live in a world that's cruel,
Where murderers, criminals and bullies rule,
People are starving and dying,
While other people are lying,
I wish people in the world would live in harmony,
Like in my world where they live calmly,
I know for sure my fantasy world's not a fact,
But the world would become a better place if it were that.

Victoria Brice (13)
Hampton Community College, Hampton

The Scarecrow

He stands there staring at the sun,
With nothing more to do,
The wind blowing through his straw-like hair,
And through the hollowness of his shoe.

As the crows and sparrows peck at him,
With all their puny might,
All he can do is stand and glare,
He can't even put up a fight.

His clothes are rags, his hair is straw,
And his hands, merely gloves on a stick,
His face is ghostly and his hat crooked,
All the children, they take the mick!

All you can do is feel so sorry for the scarecrow,
His life is so pointless, it's not there,
If you were a scarecrow, the words you would tremble are,
'Life is terribly unfair.'

Jade Lovitt (13)
Hampton Community College, Hampton

A Working World

A small hand grips the battered rake,
which starts at the wake of the day,
it doesn't stop until it near breaks.

Why should you ask does this hand work?
Throughout the day and night,
to feed the family who sees no light.

They struggle for breath and life.
    Thousands of people the same,
    living the same,
    breathing the same,
    surviving the same.
One day in the life of a 3rd World country.

Rebecca Oldham (13)
Hampton Community College, Hampton

Mum

My mum has gone missing,
Me and my sister reminiscing,
About how it used to be,
Just Mum, sister and me.
Now our mum has gone,
Our life feels like a con,
It has been two weeks now,
Feels like years but how?
It was all in good flow,
Having fun in the park,
Now we're sitting in the dark,
Thinking about our mum,
Thinking when she'll come,
A call or text would do,
We're useless without you,
You didn't even pack,
Who cares, I want you back.

Charlotte McGregor (12)
Hampton Community College, Hampton

Breaking Away

The lowest of the low,
The deepest of the deep,
I'm falling off a cliff,
That's becoming way too steep.

Literally crippling bad
And no one understands
I think I'm losing grip
Of your two hands.

My world has now turned black
Don't think that I can stay;
I think I've hit rock bottom,
I think I'm breaking away.

Yasmin White (13)
Hampton Community College, Hampton

Mixed Emotions

You are my true love
Like a free white dove
But what you lack
Is that you never come back.
I ask myself, 'Why am I alive?'
And that I should just take a dive
to the bottom of the sea
Where no one can find me.

I'm walking in the dark
And I find some sort of mark
I wonder what I see
And am I really me
I swear I'm in too deep
My life gives me the creeps
I'm fading away
Until another day.

If you only knew what I feel for you
If you only lived for me, the way I live for you
I'd be in Heaven . . . my dreams would come true
Cause all I've ever wanted is you - and you alone
All I've ever wanted is you.

Rebecca de Rose (13)
Hampton Community College, Hampton

Mirror

The mirror reflects
The picture is broken
She sees herself
Sad and lonesome.

A scared young girl
In the midst of time
With eyes so sad
Waiting for death's lonely chime.

She needs some help
Can no one see?
She wants a release
She wants to be free.

She welcomed death's cold waters
The deal was finally done
She just let go
And she was gone.

Caitlin Bartholomew (13)
Hampton Community College, Hampton

Don't Kill Me

My imprisonment gives no pleasure to my enemies
I have seen the sun deal harshly
With the dark clouds
I have been but a stem and an angry sword in a sheath
A lion in a forest or a hawk in a nest
Or a precious stone
Lying hidden in a musk box.

I'm the beginning of the end
You can see me twice in a week but not away
Once in a year, and twice in a decade
I am the one, the only one.

Amina Lunat (14)
Madani Girls' School, London

Doll!

Hair as black as evil,
Eyes as big as circles,
Speaks like a devil,
Acts like an angel.

It is the doll that which I see,
Dancing away in the joy of glee,
Planning evil in the dark,
Hoping to see the world apart.

Whispering evil to my soul,
Making me do horrendous things,
Watching every move I take,
Praying I follow the commands it makes.

Making me turn upside down,
Cramming my brain with so much shame,
Pointing towards my dream guy,
Hoping to see me forget and die.

Ripped to shreds,
Of assorted threads,
Red bracelet on the floor,
Representing evil for the more.

Away in the dark,
Locked up,
Nothing to look at,
Nothing to fuss about.

Hair as black as evil,
Eyes as big as circles,
Speaks like a devil,
Acts like an angel.

Ruhena Begum (14)
Madani Girls' School, London

Beauties Of The Sky

It is the beauty of the sky,
That lightens up your mind.
It is the beauty of the sky,
That brings life back into lifeless sights.

They stretch the wings,
And show off their lovely colours.
They glide through the sky,
Making their astonishing talents noticed.

Some hover in the sky,
Some glide through the sky,
Some dive through the sky,
Some sing songs with their elegant voices.

They come from many species,
And all with different ways of life.
They come from many types,
And amuse all the audience.

Many flock together,
Many may sound like singing,
But they worship the creator,
They beautify the view.

They make me feel happy,
With their beauty and colour.
The different colours, delicate feathers,
The birds are what I call 'beauties of the sky'.

Najmin Nahar (14)
Madani Girls' School, London

Do You Care?

Is it fair
That people are in despair?

Is it right,
Can I make it through the night?

Is it fair
The oppression, the depression?
Is it right
The fighting, the crying?

Is it fair
The anger, the hunger.
Is it right
The stabbing, the shooting.

Is it fair
The gloom, the doom.
Is it right
The fight for life?

Is it fair? No!
Is it right? No!
Do you care?

Fatima Fahia (14)
Madani Girls' School, London

Friendship

An octagon has eight ends,
A hectagon has seven ends,
A hexagon has six ends,
A pentagon has five ends,
A square has four ends,
A triangle has three ends,
A line has two ends
A life has one end
And a friendship has no end.

Afifa Khatun (14)
Madani Girls' School, London

Me And My Friends

I'm Salma and I'm so bad,
I'm so strong that I could beat your dad.
I'll learn karate, a powerful art,
The keenness of karate should come from your heart.

My friend is Nazia and she's quite cool,
To give you a warning; she ain't no fool.
She's self conscious, so get ready mate,
Get on her wrong side, it's a dangerous fate.

My friend is Sharmin and she's so clean,
Since I've met her, she's never been mean.
After some hard work, she'd never boast,
But out of all the others, she thinks the most.

My friend is Mahida and she ain't no dope,
To face my vicious friend, you need some hope.
She can be really naughty and not listen to you,
She can also be sensible, as well as you too.

Salma Ahmad (11)
Madani Girls' School, London

Beauty Of Flowers!

A garden full of beautiful flowers,
Beautifying the garden with their glamorous colours,
Scenting the garden with their gorgeous fragrance,
Who can deny the beauty of the flowers?

Swaying in the cool wind,
Blooming their wonderful colours in spring,
Making people smile as they pass by,
Who can deny the beauty of the flowers?

They come in need on birthdays and special occasions,
They come from different locations,
They beautify people's life,
Who can deny the beauty of the flowers?

Tahmina Begum (13)
Madani Girls' School, London

We Are All The Same

A lot of people are racist
They are racist for silly reasons
But they shouldn't be
If they tried to be friends they could be
Just because people are different coloured
It makes them no different
We are all the same
No matter how different we are
We are all humans
    Tall or short
    Fat or skinny
    Black or white
We are all the same
So accept us for who we are.

Rahma Noor (14)
Madani Girls' School, London

The Friendship

In life I've been through a lot,
I have been through sad and bad things,
Even suffered mad moments.
But since you have entered my life,
Everything has changed.
You are a friend in a million,
Who I never want to lose.
You hold my hand and show me right,
You are my strength,
You are my weakness.
As well as a friend I never want to let go of,
You are a friend
Who's very rare to find.
I'll hold on to you till the end,
So thank you.

Rima Begum (14)
Madani Girls' School, London

Lifeless Creature

I sit in the silence of my mind
Where all that could be heard is the wind,
Lost in thoughts I would sit,
Wondering about the purpose of life.

Sad joy,
By my loneliness I'm surrounded,
No one to share my real feeling with,
Hot ice - cold fire,
Would be my heart for life desire.

Sad is life without it,
Life with it is hard to maintain,
Can't live with it,
Nor without it.

Zineb Hamadouche (14)
Madani Girls' School, London

The Cosmic Poem

Earth, Earth spins around,
Spins around without a sound.
Mars, Mars very delicious,
But no one lives there who is vicious.
Saturn, Saturn which has a ring,
Unfortunately it has not got a king.
The moon, the moon it goes around,
The sun and Earth every day,
I don't think so, no way!
Jupiter, Jupiter the biggest about,
That's for sure, there's no doubt.
Neptune, Neptune just about medium,
It would have been better if it was a comedian.

Sadiyah Khan (11)
Madani Girls' School, London

Glory Of Sunset

I open my eyes and see the horizon forming its colours,
The exotic bright colours shining through the sea,
Making the clouds disappear,
The vibrant colours, making the sea bubble up into blazing hot fire.
As the daylight disappears,
The sunset fades into the sea,
I feel the breeze of the cool sea,
As the sun vanishes,
I feel at ease and rest in peace.
My mind settles with wonder of the pleasant sea,
I see the nature full of colour and sparkles,
One which brings me delight.
The sunset creates a summer breeze,
All of the transformation has its mystery,
A wonderful change in nature, day and night,
All sent from above.
I feel the day end with happiness and excitement,
I wait for the next sunset to bring its glory.
As night enters, it puts the sky in its moonlight form,
The twinkly stars making themselves visible now,
Now I can see the stars shining amongst each other.
I close my eyes,
I see nothing,
I fall into a deep dream.

Mansura Begum (14)
Madani Girls' School, London

Butterfly

Flying through the sky in the summer sky
Here and there, wings flutter through the breeze
My colourful wings camouflage
As I fly through the sky to catch a bit of sunshine
So here and there, far, far away
Wings are the best of all to catch a bit of sunshine.

Hanna Samin (12)
Madani Girls' School, London

One Day This Path Will End . . .

There is a road beneath my feet,
With valleys stretched beyond her,
And mountains that stand fierce and strong,
The sun that shines upon her.

Rivers flowing far and wide,
Into a world unknown,
The sky above so beautiful,
So vast and yet alone.

A single path with many turns,
With lonely tears and a happy smile,
Beneath my feet, my road goes on,
Mile after mile.

The soft blades of grass that whip my feet,
And the breeze that sings through me,
The velvet night and her silver moon,
That showers light upon me.

My path is long and yet so limited,
An end that will surely arrive,
Across an ocean reflecting the bluest sky,
My road travels, unweary and alive.

Beautiful is my world,
But more beautiful is life.

Sadeka Azad (15)
Madani Girls' School, London

The Poem

F riends are special
R eally special
E arth is full of friends
I n the Earth there are many friends
N o one can live without friends
D oing everything with friends makes you feel happy
S o don't be sad and get a friend.

Maria Uddin (13)
Madani Girls' School, London

We're All The Same

People choose between people
They quarrel over which one of them is better
Black, white, girl, boy, Muslim etc
They argue about the quality of each other
Once they said girls were rubbish
Then they said if you're black you're dirty
Now they say Muslims are a disgrace
What's next?
If you walk in a different way
You'll be treated differently
People seem to be blinded with pride
And do not see
That in fact we're all the same
No matter what your religion, colour, age
We all breathe, feel, cry and laugh
It breaks my heart to hear words such as
Nigger, terrorists and even more
Millions of people die
Just because of racism
Can't we all see that we're all the same
No matter what you are?

Hamdi Abdirahman (13)
Madani Girls' School, London

Mother

She was there when you were hers
She loves you more than the world
She cares when you're scared
She'll protect you forever and never stop
She'll buy you sweets so be sweet
She's the one that you don't want at times
But she'll want you because you're for keeps
She'll drive you to school so don't be a fool
One day you'll walk away from her, that's when she'll weep and cry
But you'll always be her baby and she'll always be your mother.

Rowshanara Islam (15)
Madani Girls' School, London

The Flower

Its clothes are its petals,
As soft as a bird's feather,
So glamorously bright in itself,
That it'll outshine the sun in the summer weather.

It'll make a dead cave sparkle,
It'll crystallise the darkest room,
A shine so bright it'll burn your eyes,
In the summer as it blooms.

Hence there are hundreds of bumblebees,
Begging for their share of honey,
Fighting for their sweet meal of pleasure,
Knowing that they'll be lucky if they got any.

Then as the night arrives,
It closed its petals and it sleeps,
Yet, its radiance is still on show,
Its beauty it always keeps.

Soon you reach out to pluck it,
Thinking that it doesn't care.
Then suddenly the pain shoots through you,
For greed there is always a fare.

Sara Mahjabin (14)
Madani Girls' School, London

Summer

The sun comes out
. . . without a doubt.

Summer has come
. . . time for some fun.

We all wanna be cool
. . . so jump in the pool.

As long as it lasts
. . . summer will always be a blast!

Abida Khatun (12)
Madani Girls' School, London

The Evil Angel

When she was born
I could have sworn,
She was a sweet
Innocent little bundle.

But when she came home
That's when it went wrong,
You'd never have known
She was a devil in clone.

All she did was cry
My mum would sigh,
And the rest of us
Would roll our eyes.

She's now older
Which is a lot scarier,
She still looks the perfect angel
When actually she's all evil.

Okay, I lied
She's not that scary,
She just annoys me
(A lot!)

Taqmina Begum Miah (14)
Madani Girls' School, London

Only You!

I would not want to be a tear in your eye,
you would wipe me away when you cry,
Not a memory of joy or your favourite cuddly toy,
Neither a diamond necklace on your neck,
You would leave me in a wreck,
What I'd really want to be would be your smile,
The reaches one's heart and travels a mile.

Humera Choudhury (12)
Madani Girls' School, London

Nature

Summer's breeze against my face
Nature's beauty has taken over me
I sit there talking to a leaf
Resting peacefully against a fence
Waiting for an amazing commence.

Every day I come and wonder
Without nature I would be a blunder
The reason I come and sit alone
Nature's beauty is my home.

They say I'm an immigrant
I don't belong here
I answer back to them
I have a beloved friend
And its name is nature.

They backbite at me
Calling me names
And once again I say
'Nature is my friend.'

Nadifa Mohamed Asman (14)
Madani Girls' School, London

Five Little Owls!

Five little owls in an old elm tree,
Fluffy and puffy as owls could be.
Blinking and winking with big round eyes,
At the big round moon that hangs in the skies.
As I passed beneath I could hear one say,
'There'll be mouse for supper, there will, today.'
Then all of them hooted, *tu-whit tu-whoo,*
Yes, mouse for supper, *hoo hoo, hoo hoo.*

Yasmin Abdulkadir D Farah (11)
Madani Girls' School, London

The Outsiders

(Based on the book 'The Outsiders' by S E Hinton)

Johnny is hunting for our football
To practise a few kicks
When a blue Mustang
Pulls up next to some chicks

Out come enough guys
To fill a hall
Johnny is so scared
He forgets about the football

Pony, Dally and Soda walking down the street
Eyeing Johnny's jacket spread over like a sheet
Looking up across the field
Seeing what they didn't wield

Running towards Johnny
Soda fell to his knees
Suppressing low moans
Begging, 'Please, please, please'

Darry comes running
Skidding to a halt
Swearing under his breath
Thinking it was his fault

Johnny now so scared
Breaks into tears
Soda just holds him
Pushes the hair back over his ears

Johnny now carries in his back pocket
A six-inch switch blade
Nobody is going to beat him like that
Now he is not afraid.

Farzana Rahman (14)
Madani Girls' School, London

My Mother

I can hear her breath vibrating in my ears
I am part of her
And she is a part of me
Her food is my food
We laugh together, we cry together
Now I can see her smiling at me
She shows me off to others
I guess she's proud of me
She cuddles me as though we rule the world
She puts pink frocks on me as though I'm a doll
She gives me whatever I need
Although I still moan and groan
She listens to me and my problems
When I cry her hands are wide open
She is a shoulder to cry on
She is my mother
And I am her daughter
I love her
And she loves me.

Noorun Nessa (15)
Madani Girls' School, London

The Prince Of The Air

He lives in my garden and sings through the year
His songs always happy his voice always clear
He's there in the summer
He's there in the spring
I wake up each morning
When I hear him sing
He's seen lots of winters, some good and some bad
But still he keeps singing, he's never seen sad
His breast is bright red, there's brown on his wings
And I always feel better whenever he sings
It makes me so happy to know that he's there
My friend, the robin, the prince of the air.

Sakina Delli (13)
Madani Girls' School, London

Life

Life is like a chain of events
Life has sad times and happy times
When summer comes and says goodbye
Soon winter comes, soon it'll be gone
This is life for young and old
While old people's funerals start running
Newborn babies are born
Middle-aged people rush to work
While young children work hard at school
And those yobs who make themselves become fools
Summer holidays come and the people are off work
They book the plane and travel to countries
They bake themselves like potatoes in an oven
On the nice, sunny, hot beaches
Aren't they having so much fun?
So soon those people return to work and start working hard
You see this is life for young and old
And summer came and waved
And winter's on its way round
You see this is life like a chain of events
Whether it's happy or sad
Sooner or later the old will die
And a new life will be born.

Anisah Elafia (15)
Madani Girls' School, London

Autumn

Leaves rustling happily,
Falling off their mother tree,
Squirrels dancing up and down,
Gathering nuts for around the town,
Nightingales building nests,
Creating a habitat for them to rest,
Crisp golden flakes covering the earth,
Making way for *winter's* birth.

Sara Bihi (11)
Madani Girls' School, London

Criminal!

Once in my life I was so happy,
I had my family, standing right beside me.
The boys like Shah, Jay and Big Joe,
My so-called friends - who were actually foes.
They made it look so nice and easy,
Robbing some old woman named Ms Jersay.
I never knew what I was doing was so wrong,
Cause every time I did - I felt so strong.
Shah would snatch the bag,
Then Jay would take out a fag.
Me and Joe spent the money,
On anything we wanted, mostly jewellery.
But all my life I spent doing this,
Now I'm in a cell, all I can do is reminisce.
My life, really ends here,
Inside four walls, which feel like raging fire.
I live each day pinching my back,
Thinking, *if only I could go back.*
But all I can do is just stare at a glass,
Praying to God, 'Forgive my past!'

Reshma Begum (13)
Madani Girls' School, London

The Gymnast

She jumps steadily with pride
Her eyes gleaming as blue as ever
Showing that she is clever
She hops on the wall
Without a single fall
Her bodysuit gleaming white
In the very dark night
Cheers of the audience rise
And then, to the judges' startled cries
She makes her final leap
And then lands in a total heap.

Aisha Yusuf (11)
Madani Girls' School, London

Words From The Heart

Why is the season sealed with love?
Whose moonlit eyes do I foretell in every beaming star?

Why is the azure swelled with desire?
Whose tune is whistling in my ears?
Whose echoes are encountering in my feelings?

Why is the sun excited with passion?
Whose illuminated face do I visualise in every blushing blossom?
Whose fragrance is swaying with my dreams?
Whose cloud of exuberance is embracing my path?

Why is the wind coiling with remembrance?
Whose arrival is predicted in my soul?

Why is the season sealed with desire
With passion
With remembrance
And love?

Noorjahan Begum (15)
Madani Girls' School, London

Summertime

Summer is very warm
With the flowers bursting
And a new season starting
The sun is shining high
It's time for ice cream
Summer is splendid

Summer is beautiful
All the birds are singing
A new life is beginning
The stars are shining
The sky is bright and blue
Summer is just splendid.

Halima Khatun (11)
Madani Girls' School, London

What's Up?

What's up?
Looking at all the hardship
What's wrong?
Watching all the fighting.

What's up?
Seeing all the bodies
What's wrong?
Your mother, your father and your sisters too.

What's up?
Hearing all the crying
What's wrong?
Hearing all the screaming

What's up?
Feeling all the sadness
What's wrong?
Feeling all the distress

What's up?
Everything!
What's wrong?
Everything!
I'm not complaining.

Huda Fahia (12)
Madani Girls' School, London

Flowers

Flowers are happy,
Flowers are sad,
They don't stink like a baby's nappy,
They're not like bullies, all rough and bad,
They have feelings just like you and me,
Buzzing from one to another is a bumblebee,
Not all just a beautiful life, they also go through pain,
The best thing about flowers
Is they're all unique.

Sharmin Nizam (12)
Madani Girls' School, London

I Wonder, I Wonder What The World Has For Me

I wonder, I wonder what the world has for me.
I wonder why I'm so alone,
And I wonder why I cry this morning all alone,
I walk on the street and see no one cares about me.
I wonder, I wonder what the world has for me.
Am I just inferior to the world,
Or am I just another species?
Or maybe I just don't belong here.
Whatever my fate has for me I hope it's good.
I wonder, I wonder what the world has for me.
My mother just curses me, my father I don't know.
I wonder, I wonder what the world has for me.
I dream of being a doctor but that's up to fate.
I wonder, I wonder what the world has for me.
Today I lie awake crying wishing that the world has something for me,
Children are victims of abuse,
They cry while no one seems to notice,
So many organisations, so many people but they still don't know.
I wonder, I wonder what the world has for these children.
The government calls itself a freedom fighter while their children cry.
I wonder, I wonder what the world has for these children.
But for the meantime I'll pray and cry till someone notices me.

Leyla Bulhan (15)
Madani Girls' School, London

Love

For love is romantic
And romantic is red
Love is in our heart
From the day it starts

Love is in the air
Love is so true
No matter where you are
I'll still love you.

Rashida Begum (12)
Madani Girls' School, London

Best Friends Forever!

As the years pass
and we grow apart,
I want you to know
that you're in my heart.

You helped me through problems,
Through things good and bad,
You helped me keep smiling
when I was sad.

You helped me when I cried,
You made me stay strong,
How will I love
when you are gone?

And where the years take us
no place is too far,
We will think of each other
wherever we are . . .

You're a wonderful person
with a good heart to lend
and I want you to know . . .
you're my best friend.

Tasnim Khanom (12)
Madani Girls' School, London

Friendship

Friends are special people,
they'll always stay with you,
like buddies and supporters,
they're loyal, kind and true.
Never take advantage
and never let them down,
a friend indeed is a friend in need.

Shefali Begum (11)
Madani Girls' School, London

The Mermaid

She swings her silvery tail,
While she sits on a rock,
Brushing her beautiful fair hair.
The shells she collects are glistening, so rare.
She swims underwater,
Where the prince awaits her,
In the fantasy land,
Where the sea beds are covered with sand,
And the walls are made of crystals,
It's where the prince rules.
She swims underwater,
Where he awaits her,
Her beautiful face too good to miss,
He touches her cheeks and gives her a gentle kiss.

Marjuka Karima (11)
Madani Girls' School, London

Raise Your Soul

Vision, vision, religion
See your way
It's hard to say
Vision, vision, religion

Listen to the heart
Build up the chart
Sing your song
Sing your song

Pray to the Lord
Raise your soul
Shoot the ball
Score a goal.

Tahmina Ahmed (12)
Madani Girls' School, London

Love And Its Mysterious Ways

The years have quickly gone by,
Since the day I saw you catch my eye,
I did not have the courage to speak,
My mouth was so dry, I was ready to drink from a creek.

As soon as I saw you, I knew it was true,
My heart was light, it felt like it flew,
Unfortunately my love was far greater than my courage,
So I kept tight-lipped as I pathetically always do.

This is the lowest I can go,
Writing a poem that doesn't even flow,
I am the worst of the worst,
My love for you is like a curse.

A curse in the way that you are my head,
A blessing in the way you are in my heart,
As I lay looking at the ceiling on my bed,
I feel like I am being prickled with love darts.

So, nowadays, I still think of you,
You're still in my heart,
The boy I saw at the Kwik-E-Mart.

Yasmin Jama (14)
Madani Girls' School, London

The Ladybird

She goes through all the flowers,
Giving it one last shower,
Wrapping it around in a silver ribbon,
So that it's nice and hidden,
Until one comes and gazes,
And goes into a world that's beautiful and full of daisies,
Ladybird gives it one last look,
Then says goodbye to it,
Oh! How sad it is,
For what a ladybird she is.

Tanya Fateha Sultana (12)
Madani Girls' School, London

Exploring Something New

I'm standing all alone
An oasis
Around me a sandstorm of chatter
'How are you?'
'I'm fine!'
'How was your holiday?'
'Great fun!'
'I've missed you since we left.'
Running through my mind a stream -
Natasha, Rachael, Lucy, Katie -
Wondering what it's like for them.

I have always been a tall palm tree
Surrounded by friends, but now
The sands swirl closer and closer
I'm left to feel like I've shrunk
And I stand still as a stone.

Courage, I need courage
To speak to that sparkling brown-eyed girl
Standing in her own oasis.

Will friendship blossom on the new path
Lying ahead of us?

Nazia Ahmed (15)
Madani Girls' School, London

Runaway Train

Its vicious roar is heard from miles away
Its mysterious eyes glow bright and set the area alight
Smoke pours out of the funnel volcano
Its snaky body twists and turns
Its enormous belly grumbles and groans
It unleashes an ear-piercing screech
It comes to a final halt
Colonies of people march off the mechanical creature.

Aisha Warren (11)
Madani Girls' School, London

Rainbow!

When I woke up in the morning, what did I see?
I looked out the window, my face filled with glee.
Seven different colours, all in a row,
I thought to myself, *could this be a rainbow?*

A substance made out of rain and sunshine,
Oh, how I wish this rainbow could be mine.

A fable story was told,
At the end of the rainbow, there lies a pot of gold,
Could this be true,
Or are these all lies too?
Just like the leprechauns,
Who all come out before dawn.

I wonder how all those colours get there,
It'll be more colourful to wear,
All different shades,
Too unique to be made.

But rainbow, please don't go away,
Stay there until another day,
You make summer come into me,
And make me feel like a wild bumblebee.

But the rainbow did not reply,
And you do not have to ask why,
For the rainbow had gone away,
Leaving me to wonder for another day.

Parveen Begum (13)
Madani Girls' School, London

Summer

Its blistering wind makes you sweat
A playful and joyful time for kids
It is a time for them to make the most of fun
Freshens their minds with a long-lasting holiday
Seasides packed with enjoying voices
Delicious food bundled in baskets ready for picnics
It is a pleasant season that only comes once a year.

Fresh smells from new flowers
Daffodils, daisies, bluebells, buttercups everywhere
All colourful and gaudy, attracting butterflies
The scorching sun brightens up summer
Ice cream van zooming across the road
Child by child stopping for ice cream
Which may refresh them
Summer season is pleasing
Its weather is just so delightful.

Khadijah Begum (15)
Madani Girls' School, London

My Loving Cousin

She was just like all the other babies
Smiling and cheerful
But one day our dream shattered in pieces
When we realised that the world was mute to her
Will she ever be able to listen to the birds singing?
Will she ever be able to listen to our lullabies?
All these difficult questions wandering through our minds
Thanks to Allah and with the help of modern technology
She is able to hear as much as we can now.

Sumayyah Faridah Hussain (11)
Madani Girls' School, London

Our Teacher Lost Her Voice Today

It happened to be on a Monday morning,
The children had arrived as the day was dawning,
And then suddenly appeared our teacher,
Who seemed to have an unusual feature.

Suddenly the silence broke,
As she came out with an awful croak,
And then Joe Henry piped up,
'I think she has lost her voice.'

So kids everywhere looked under tables,
Chairs and inside books,
Until she started to give us those looks,
Finally Jason Plum said,
'You can have my voice instead.'

Sharmila Haque (12)
Madani Girls' School, London

Jeeves

There was a man called Jeeves
He ate a lot of Cheddar cheese
He walked into town with a broken arm
A souvenir of a fight with a pig on the farm
The pig was strong and fat
His mate the cat helped the pig to fight with Jeeves
And put pepper up his nose to make Jeeves sneeze
Everyone in the town loves to tease Jeeves
His mum teases and always pays the fees.

Seinab Warsama (12)
Madani Girls' School, London

My Beloved

A person we had the shoulder to cry on,
We always knew that everything
Was going to be fine when he was around,
He also was a helpful hand,
He always had a smile on his face,
To make everyone happy was his joy,
He made love in everyone's heart,
He was always there for a talk or a cuppa.

He always was around and never down,
He was kind and helpful,
But unfortunately he left us and died,
His words are still vibrating in my ears,
Our lives are empty now and we are without him.

Every moment he is being missed,
And he was my very beloved uncle.

Jamila Khan (14)
Madani Girls' School, London

Smoking

Why do people kill themselves
With just one puff of smoke
Whilst they could be enjoying themselves
And eating fruit with Coke.

Do they do it just for a dare
Or do they think it's cool?
But in reality
They're just a walking fool.

Do they do it just for fun
Or don't they have a clue
That the next day
There'll be nothing left of *you?*

Farhiya Abdirahman (12)
Madani Girls' School, London

Wintertime Nightmare!

The rain falls heavily from the sky,
Pitter-patter, pitter-patter,
As the sky growls angrily up so high.

The ground shakes with the rolls of thunder,
Clap, bang, clap, bang,
While the animals hide in their houses down under.

When will this endless rain stop?
Tick-tock, tick-tock,
It goes on dripping like a wet and soaked mop.

The rivers are cleansed with this sweet shower,
Swish-swosh, swish-swosh,
And the sea's shaken with almighty power.

Ding-a-ling, ding-a-ling,
The alarm rings,
Phew, that was a real scare!

Tamanna Mukith (12)
Madani Girls' School, London

Chocolates

C hocolate is velvety-rich and sweet
H aving some chocolate, it's a treat
O h there's so many chocolates, have some for fun
C runchie, Galaxy, try more than one
O ne little bite and you'll want some more
L ick the wrapper that's what I adore
A t the end the chocolate's so smooth
T ake a bite, it makes your heartache soothe
E veryone eats chocolate, it's a total delight
S omething you hate and love with all your might.

Farhana Yasmin (14)
Madani Girls' School, London

Man

Man is pleasant,
he looks after the Earth,
and the animals,
he feeds the young,
and protects the old,
he nurses the ill,
and provides the needy.
Man surely is pleasant.

Man is pleasant,
he protects the environment,
and controls his movement,
man helps his neighbours,
he loves those close to him,
and hates those that hurt them.
Surely man is pleasant.

Man is pleasant,
he houses the poor,
and pets the hurt,
he hushes the crying baby,
and brings a smile to faces of the old,
with delight brings a twinkle to the eye of a child.
Man surely is pleasant, is it not so?

Man is pleasant to all,
except one.
He hates one and would not spare his life,
if he could.
But surely man is more pleasant,
than to do this, is it not so?

Who is this one,
that is so bad,
that pleasant man could not spare life?
Is it a monster?
Surely not because man is pleasant to all.

This one that pleasant man hates
is man.
One equal with himself,
one with some ideas and thoughts,
yet man hates man,
so is man really pleasant?

Does pleasant mean hate
or is hate evil?
Is man pleasant when he
hates?
Is it pleasant to hate and kill,
or is it pleasant to love and care?

Is man really pleasant or is he just evil?

Adna Duran (15)
Madani Girls' School, London

Teachers

Roses are red,
Violets are grey,
I'll give you a pretty card
And you'll give me an A.

For teaching me lessons,
And helping my knowledge grow,
All I want to say is
You're the best teacher I know.

I wanted an A because I don't think I've done well at all,
I did an incredibly hard exam yesterday,
This girl saw me looking and I said, 'Don't tell.'
She didn't!
For she knew I was going to bully her baby doll Mel!

Bilan Djama (13)
Madani Girls' School, London

Football!

Football is my favourite sport,
It's the best of the lot.
Football has different teams,
And they all have certain themes.

Man United are the best,
Wanna be like them, gotta pass the test.
They don't ever mess up games, lest,
They should be known as lower than the rest.

Man United know how to cruise,
Arsenal only know how to lose.
The ugly Gunners think they're cool,
But they make themselves such a fool.

When Man U win, the Gunners accuse,
But cos the Devils rule, you can't refuse.
Arsene Wenger loves to fight,
But Sir Alex Ferguson is out of sight.

Abeda Khanom (13)
Madani Girls' School, London

Friends Forever!

Friends can last forever,
Like a flower stuck together.
The petals of a flower growing closer,
The love of a friend getting sweeter.
Observing the love of one's heart,
Cannot make friendship grow apart.
That's what you call
Friends forever!

Karima Meksem (14)
Madani Girls' School, London

Untitled

I reminisce about the day
when I saw you for the first time
I looked into those shiny, extraordinary eyes
that eloped with mine.

Each and every day
I would look to the skies
at the single star that lights my lonely way
and yearn for the beauty and grace that lies within.

I must watch from afar
and long for the silk-touched, striking
angel that you are.

My affection will go nowhere
it will always be with me
I'll hold you in my heart
and hope that one day it could be.

You have this beauty . . .
wild and free
but the backdrop of reality is that
you're not all for me.

For there are others out there
who want to share your grace
acting as if they care
wanting to see your face.

But yet I still wonder who you are
you're the inspiration for someone
who wanted to do art.

And still to this day
I'm hoping waiting and hoping
some more
I'll meet someone like you again.

Raha Noor (14)
Madani Girls' School, London

The Lady In The Mirror

I saw a lady in the mirror
I thought she wasn't there
I reached out to touch her
But then she disappeared.

I saw her on my walk that day
Her eyes were sad and filled with tears
That dripped into the snow
I walked towards her
But when I looked up she was gone.

I saw her when I woke that day
She stared at me in such a strange way
She seemed so sad, so cold and silent
And at times she looked so frightened.

At night as I slept I saw her in my dreams
She stared at me with those cold, sad eyes
I felt as if they were cutting through me.

But one morning I woke to hear the birds singing
In all their morning glory.

I stood and looked into the mirror
And there she stood before me
Her face was bright and filled with happiness
As she took a step towards me.

She stood there smiling
Her cheeks as red as roses
Then she took my hand
And led me out into the bright spring morning.

Safiya Reynolds-Myers
Madani Girls' School, London

War

My world felt peaceful
under the clear blue sky,
the faintest of bullets
fired one after another.

My world started shattering,
there was no time for stopping.
I run, my footsteps becoming faster,
bang, bang, bang, bang.

Boom - the bomb has exploded,
I can hear people screaming,
I can see the flames glowing,
my heart is pounding,
I must keep on running, running.

Roar, roar - the cannons have fired,
I can hear them rumbling and raving,
I can see the buildings erupting,
the flames howling and histling,
and I still keep on running, running.

My world was returning,
my heart was still beating,
I am still living, surviving,
I can't hear the screaming or shouting,
nor the howling and histling.

The sky was not blue yet,
but I know I still have hope left,
I will find peace and salvation,
for my country and my people,
by doing justice between all creation.

Sheba Khanom (13)
Madani Girls' School, London

The Panther

Gliding through the moonlight,
In and out of the dark shadows,
Braver than the mightiest knight,
Even without any shiny armour.

Patiently waiting silently,
To catch his enemy off guard,
Pouncing off the ground lightly,
Taking his prey down.

No one can equal their strength to him,
He shows no mercy to anyone,
Not his friends nor his enemy,
He is independent.

Beware of this beastly creature,
You don't want to run into him,
If he gets you, there's no escape,
For he is the mighty panther.

Ismatara Nipa (13)
Madani Girls' School, London

The Miracle Called Friendship

There's a miracle called friendship
That dwells between the hearts
You don't know how it happens
Or when it gets its start
But the happiness it brings you
Always gives a special lift
And you realise that
Friendship is life's most precious gift.

Sabina Begum (13)
Madani Girls' School, London

My Mum

You have loved me, cared for me, and nurtured me,
And I have been made to feel so special in this family,
Yet it's hard for me to think,
How it is I may repay you,
The way you comfort me, the way you love me,
And everything else you do,
You have been through hardship and suffered much pain,
But from all of this, what is it that you gain?
I promise that I'll love you,
Stay with you and be your security,
Although we have our arguments and I am very witty,
But we both know you are mine for keeps and I am yours forever,
I wish you only happiness and that we should stay strong together,
For there is no better gift
Than to be given you as a mother,
No one can be as equal as you, not my sister or my brother,
But most of all *I love you.*

Aneesa Ahmed (13)
Madani Girls' School, London

What Do You Think?

Walking down the street
I thought to myself,
Am I ugly? Am I pretty?
What do you think?

Opinions, opinions,
I've had it all
Just say the truth
That's what I want most of all.

Do I look cute in my suit?
It's time to go
You better tell me more
Than you know.

Syeda Nadiya Begum (12)
Madani Girls' School, London

Chocolate

So brown, so sweet,
Melting in my mouth,
Trickling down my chin,
Heading towards south.

So rich, so tasty,
Dissolving on my tongue,
Swimming through a tunnel,
Going through my lungs.

So mesmerising, so mouth-watering,
Making my insides burn,
Turning the cave into a dreamland,
Causing my mind to do a U-turn.

Yet so mysterious,
So sensual,
Functioning along my brain,
Carrying with it so much potential.

So nutritious, so scrumptious,
Making my mouth water,
Some of it escaping,
As it's growing shorter and shorter.

So brown, so sweet,
Melting in my mouth,
Trickling down my chin,
Heading towards south.

Nazia Begum (13)
Madani Girls' School, London

The Friendless Loner

I am a stranger,
I am always there,
Why don't you want to know me?
I am not evil, I am not insane,
I am a stranger,
I am not going to hurt you,
Why don't you recognise me?
Come talk to me,
I am not a bomb, I am not stupid,
I am a stranger,
Why do you all laugh at me?
I am not a creep, I am not a weirdo,
I am a stranger,
Well only to you.
Come closer, get to know me,
I am so lonely, I have nobody,
I can be your friend,
Even if I am a stranger.
Can't you see me?
Why not come over?
Come and see me.
Why are you all so cruel?
Just because I am a stranger.

Tasnia Khatun (13)
Madani Girls' School, London

Friendship

It's good to have a special friend
to talk to when I'm blue,
life would not be half as nice
if I did not have you.
I always know when things go right,
my happiness you'll share,
and I know too there's few like you,
true friends are very rare.

Marzia Begum (13)
Madani Girls' School, London

Grief From The Grave

Oh how I plead for life
As thou taketh my body,
Thou places me in the darkness of the pit without light.
I cry to thee, 'Don't leave me,' but no souls hear me.
The darkness so strange, I look at my right, no mother,
At my left, no wife.
Thou taketh 40 steps, angel approaches me,
I cry for mother, I cry for wife with grief and fright.
Now the light I see is the blazing, glowing red eyes
Squinting like a mole to see the flames coming from its mouth.
Questions start striking me like thundering bolts of light,
Which fills the grave with more grief and fright.
My throat tightens and now squeaking like a mouse I answer them,
'Ahh! Ahh! I don't know, I don't know!'
Another bolt strikes me and says,
'You wasted your wealth,
Wasted your youth, with pride and lust,
Now ye may taste more grief and sorrow,
Till the day of tomorrow.'
So now I say to you all,
Do good deeds of all that shall lighten and brighten one's soul.
So shall the garden of bliss be yours,
Alas, don't be like me who sees darkness of all,
And the snakes of all kind,
Striking me from dusk till dawn . . .

Fatima Begum (12)
Madani Girls' School, London

Things I Hate To Do!

I am writing this poem,
So don't think you're going.
The worst thing is at home,
Because I never ever find my comb.
My bedroom gets messy, from bottom to top,
And I end up having to clean it up.

I really, really, really hate it,
But my mum would shout if I stop and sit.
I hate to eat some fishes,
Because I will end up doing the dishes.
My mum then starts calling me,
And tells me to make her a cup of tea.

Even though I hate it,
I go to put on the kettle,
And I try to calm and settle.

I hate doing my sister's job,
Which is doing the washing up.
Anyway she'll shout and scream,
And every morning she puts on cream.

I hate to get up early in the morning,
Because it is really, really boring.
We have to go to school,
Which isn't very cool.

When we walk up the stairs,
We have to go in pairs.
I walk into the classroom,
And I end up having to broom.

I'm afraid I have to go,
But I will be back though,
So be aware of the bear!

Hannah Meksem (12)
Madani Girls' School, London

Fire!

I am big, I am scary
I am hot and red
I slither through your skin
And make them rot

You scream and shout
But there's no way of stopping me
You hurt and cry
But that's my job to make you scared.

'Help!' is your plea
My flames make you suffer
If you want my name, here it is . . .
My name is Fire!

Husna Khatun (13)
Madani Girls' School, London

Flowers

Flower, flower
Big and bright,
God has created you
So perfect in height.
You open up
In the morning light,
And close your petal
In the dark black night.
It's so amazing
How God made you,
Where he got the brains,
I don't have a clue.
We thank God
Every night and day,
For making our lives
So beautiful day by day.

Jahanara Begum (12)
Madani Girls' School, London

Forever Friends

Forever friends
Never ends
It's always happy
And never snappy.

Forever friends
Never bends
It's always together
Soft like a feather.

Forever friends
Always sends
Magic happiness all the way round
That has a tingling sound.

Forever friends
Always lends
That's full of stars just like above
With stuff that's beautiful like a dove.

Forever friends
Always mends
The circle that was always there
And calls the magic to come near.

Halima Begum (13)
Madani Girls' School, London

School!

The school is as high as a mansion
It looks like a fountain
It is made out of bricks
And books are marked with ticks.

The school has three layers
Where the students do their prayers
The staffroom is where the teachers are
When you go knocking all they say is, 'Tarrah!'

Fatimah Temitope Awesu (13)
Madani Girls' School, London

Love Poem

Be mine forever
And I'll be yours too
We are so good together
I'll always love you.

I'll bring you roses
In the pouring rain
Living without you
Is driving me insane.

You are everything to me
Someone I can count on
Someone I love
With all my heart.

Each dream of mine
Begins and ends
With a loving thought of you
Important part of everything I do.

Helena Ahmed (13)
Madani Girls' School, London

Friendship

A friend is someone who believes in you,
Who believes in what you say and do.
Who remembers you night and day,
And never lets you go astray.
A friend is someone who's always there,
And makes you feel special and rare.
Without a friend we are incomplete,
Nobody but you deserves a special treat.

Shahida (13)
Madani Girls' School, London

Our World

Our world has soaring mountains
The deep oceans sing with the storms
Our rain springs down like a water fountain
The rocks modify in different forms.

Our sky is streaming in the sunlight
The stars gleam in the shadows
Our trees grow tall with all their might
The desert animals live deep down below.

Our moon comes out every night
The smiles on our face
Our eyes shine at every sight
It makes us think the world is a . . .
Beautiful place.

Rayhana Khanom (13)
Madani Girls' School, London

Football

I play football cos it's fun
Even if there is no sight of the sun
If you play football you'll be fit
All you need to do is get a ball and kick it.

Tackle right, tackle left, dodge past and score!
Watching people standing there is a real bore
If you play football you get a lot of fans
Just like C Ronaldo and the rest of his clan.

People think being goalie is really sad
But just wait and see, it's the best time you've ever had
If you get tired just have tea in a cup
No matter what happens don't give up.

Football is everything
And easy like string
Move your skinny legs and get down to business.

Rahima Begum (13)
Madani Girls' School, London

Going To School At 9am

Going to school at nine, what do I do?
Brush my teeth,
Comb my hair,
Change my clothes, don't look,
Don't you dare.
Time for nails - pink or blue?
What do you think,
Turquoise shoes?
Looking in the mirror,
Where's your opinion?
Model suits me,
No time for gossip.
2 minutes to go,
I rush out the door,
Running, skipping.
Finally here at last,
So laters now, gotta go, I'll see you at home at 4.

Sheikh Mursana Begum (13)
Madani Girls' School, London

The Mermaid

Her golden curls shine like the sun,
In her turquoise parlour she has so much fun,
Everyone knows her for her beautiful face,
And so much beauty she puts in one case,
Many faces she turns into shining stars,
But her own beauty can be seen near and far,
In any condition, shape or race
You can always recognise the face of . . . the mermaid.

Kaha Yusuf (12)
Madani Girls' School, London

I Am A Samurai

My goal is to succeed
My way is honour and pride
My life is hard
But I only gain
For I am a samurai.

My sen-sei trains me
My instincts lead me
I travel as fast as lightning
But my past lingers
For I am a samurai.

I befriend the shadows
They are my only hope
I confide in good
But bad is not far behind
For I am a samurai.

Swift and sharp are my moves
Gentle and pure is my mind
Slow and steady is my breath
But fast and deadly is my pace
For I am a samurai.

My missions are terrifying
I battle for my heart and soul
My sword is my shield
But fear is my enemy
For I am a samurai.

My journey leads me
My path is narrowing
I am faced with hatred
But light is ahead
For I am a samurai.

Maariyah Syeda (13)
Madani Girls' School, London

Friendship

Roses are red
Violets are blue
Nothing is harder
Than to find a friend like you.

Country to country is easy to find
A friend like you is hard to find.

Roses are red
Violets are blue
I couldn't wish
For a better friend than you.

Tree to tree is hard to climb
A friend like you is hard to find.

Roses are red
Violets are blue
Nobody could ever
Replace a friend like you.

Friendship is a circle
That is bound with love and care.

Rahnoma Sultana (13)
Madani Girls' School, London

Love Is Not Love And Love Is What?

Love is not love if we separate,
Love is not love if we fight or hate,
Love is not love if there is no trust,
Love is not love if everything's rushed,
Love is not love if you don't care for one another,
Love is not love if you don't have time for your sister or brother.

Love is what we need,
Love is what we should breath,
Love is what we should receive,
Love is what we should believe,
Love is in every living thing,
Imagine all the happiness love could bring,
Love is always on the rise,
Love should be in everyone's eyes,
Love could turn a heart to gold,
Love could turn a heart cold,
Love is from the true heart,
Love is life till death do us part.

Yinka Lawal (13)
St James Independent School for Senior Boys, Twickenham

Loneliness

It is like being locked away
No one speaks to you
You can't escape from it
You feel unwanted
No one seems to see or care about your needs
You feel like life's not worth living
No one knows you
You're stuck
You can't do anything
You feel useless
Never choose the path of loneliness.

William Ford (14)
St James Independent School for Senior Boys, Twickenham

Sonnet 666

Every man has the power to strike death,
Although most are also somewhat wiser.
Knowing the blunder of ceasing man's breath,
A man would shun the path of a miser.
The man who forgets his gift of wisdom,
And breaks the laws of man and God the same,
Will be kept from the Heavenly Kingdom,
And till Doomsday, disgraced will be his name:
Thus learning his harsh lesson evermore.
Death will have his rightful retribution,
Just as in life man is punished by law.
Instead the wise make a contribution:
He creates another, with his lover,
And soon wishes he was even smarter.

Will Purves (13)
St James Independent School for Senior Boys, Twickenham

My Dreams

I've always wanted to fly,
But never had time to try.
I've always felt lonely in this world,
To me, it's always dead.

I always wanted to be strong,
But this dream is stupid and wrong.
I wanted to be an eagle in the air,
Flying high with my eyes everywhere.

I've always wanted to be a soldier,
Carrying my big gun on my shoulder.
These dreams are so wild,
Wild like a baby child.

I've always wanted to be an honest man:
This has always been my lifelong plan,
My most wanted desire,
My life's fire.

Aaron Kler (13)
St James Independent School for Senior Boys, Twickenham

An Orphan

An orphan is a lonely child
Who has nowhere else to go
But when the times do get low
Time seems to fly by so very slow.

An orphan is a person
Who has sadly had an unlucky life
Whose parents have gone
And has to have done
A most treacherous journey
Through pain and strife.

If you witness it
You'll know it's not a game
Its life is lame
But then again there's always
A good side to things
To be lifted out of sorrow
On the back of an angel's wings.

The pain will go away
Maybe today or every day
When the child's life will end
The dark barrier will come to bend
The other way for good,
And then, it will mend.

Pawel Madej-Brunsz (13)
St James Independent School for Senior Boys, Twickenham

How Wondrous It Would Be

How wondrous it would be,
To see the universe unfold,
The stars and planets created from nothing,
Right before our eyes,
You and I watching the beginning of the world.

How wondrous it would be,
To see the animals evolve,
Step by step into their present forms,
Right before our eyes,
You and I watching the wonders of creation.

How wondrous it would be,
To see the ancient battles,
The epic stories that remain untold,
Heroes dying with their fellow men,
Right before our eyes,
You and I watching history write itself.

How wondrous it would be,
To see the great men and women that have been,
Expressing their feelings and beliefs,
Seeking out the truth, and sharing it with others,
Right before our eyes,
You and I watching heroes from all through time.

How wondrous it would be,
To see the end of all things,
The world return to its original form,
The souls of all being weighed and measured,
Right before our eyes,
You and I watching the apocalypse.

How wondrous it is now,
To sit upon this grassy hill,
A warm breeze blowing by, as the flickering colours of the setting sun,
Fill the sky, and our minds flicker back to think of peaceful times,
The beauty of the world,
Right before our eyes,
You and I, hand in hand, at the closing of the day.

Charles Wood (14)
St James Independent School for Senior Boys, Twickenham

Darkness

With his cloak
Darkness creeps,
While half the world
Is asleep.
The other half,
A lovely day,
Taken by darkness
And locked away.
Blind as he is,
He knows where to go,
And in his selection
Are rain and snow.
Running in circles
All night and day,
He has no companions
And wants none anyway.
His strides are silent,
But wherever he dwells he pulls out black,
For that is his favourite colour,
And he leaves it all over his track.

Omar Mousa (13)
St James Independent School for Senior Boys, Twickenham

Monday Morning

My alarm goes off and my headache starts
No rest for the wicked, no rest for my heart
I roll out of bed and into the cold
I pick up my sandwich and pick off the mould
I stick it in my bag and get ready for school
This is Monday morning and it just isn't cool

I get to the platform at ten past eight
I'd better hurry up or I might be late
I'm standing in the station in the pouring rain
It's half past eight and where's my bloody train?

I get to Richmond and take a H22
The tyre gets a puncture, I don't know what to do
I get to school and the head is waiting for me
He grabs my neck and I can't breathe
'Please Sir, I'm not to blame!'
'I don't care, it's a red card, don't be late again'
I turn around and see a queue
He grabs the next boy and says, 'What's your excuse?'

Matthew Balmforth (14)
St James Independent School for Senior Boys, Twickenham

Under The Stairs

The cupboard under the stairs is my thinking place,
I like to go there when I need some space.
When I'm there I have a sense of gloom,
It's nothing like your average room.
There are many spiders and cobwebs too,
Lots of boots and a smelly old shoe.
In this place I like to sit,
Then lie down and dream a bit.
I think about the world outside,
Oh so big and oh so wide.
It's nothing special, it's just a place,
It's where I go to get some space.

Arthur Lawrence (14)
St James Independent School for Senior Boys, Twickenham

Lake Geneva, Switzerland: August 2nd 2000

1800hrs

I sat by the waters, drinking the view,
Sucking in the noises, the lapping of the deep, dark blue.
content stroked my forehead; its fingers were cool,
Nearby, in the lake, the fish were at school.
And all the while, I sat there, soaking it in,
My feet in the water, my hand on the chin.

1900hrs

The sun was now setting, its breath on the Alps,
The reds and oranges, massaging snowy scalps.
Not needing to move I watched its retreat,
And to me this fine feeling may never repeat.
With hope in my heart, I'll go there again,
Some feeling described, the bliss, I cannot explain.

William Nichols (14)
St James Independent School for Senior Boys, Twickenham

The Navigator's Eye

As the moon grinned at the boat,
With its bright crescent smile;
And the water's wrath grew old
But had enough to last a while.
The navigator's eye grew cold
And lost its weary shine:
Looking at the vast ocean
And its everlasting motion.
Then his eyes turn to the sky;
Dark and starless without a cry.
Then the clouds clashed,
With their fists held high
Letting loose their burden
Over the navigator's eye.
Then slowly the eye fell asleep
Dooming the boat to sleep in the deep.

Suchin Mehrotra (12)
St James Independent School for Senior Boys, Twickenham

The Concert

A swollen mass of people all pushing and shoving to get inside
the auditorium,
Moans and groans as they see the long lines to enter the arena floor.
Even though they moan and groan, the excitement is electric,
Excitement builds as they one by one find their best place.

Suddenly a lone voice fills the room and all goes quiet -
the announcement.
The crowd erupt, but on stage nothing, no people, no light, no sound.
A feeble, quiet sound of a lone guitar drifts out from the dark stage,
Next an explosion of lights blind everyone, fireworks shoot up
into the night sky.
Drums begin to methodically pound, beat by beat, cymbal by cymbal,
The feeble guitar now rocks, high note, low note, screeching chords.
The crowd cheer, jump and throw floating inflatables amongst
themselves,
The singer becomes the only voice, joined by every other voice
in the crowd.

At the last song - the finale, that song fades and fades to a slow
long silence,
The lights grow dimmer and dimmer eventually to darkness.
Slowly the crowd start to chant for more and more, chanting faster
and faster,
Eventually the lights explode back on; the group file back onto
the stage,
The encore begins, harder than before, louder than before,
brighter than before.

When all is over and the band have bid everyone goodnight
with thanks,
The lights die out, but the feeling does not, remembering
the best moments
The excitement of the concert carries the crowd home, by bus,
by taxi, by car.

Nicholas North (13)
St James Independent School for Senior Boys, Twickenham

The Trainer

I'm a size nine,
And I'm Nike.
I'm white with grey and blue additions.
He's 13, the boy whose feet consider me his,
Once my laces are tied up off we go.
When I'm on this boy's feet,
I see the park,
All the people and shoes enjoying themselves.
We then run and play football,
And I kick the ball as far as I can,
All the way to my fellow shoe.
We then go and meet a dog,
And I'm slobbered with a dog kiss.
I'm so glad that my owner adopted me,
Now I can see the world and I'm not stuck on a shelf in Footlocker.

Casper Ponnampalam (13)
St James Independent School for Senior Boys, Twickenham

The Swing

I felt as if I was flying,
I went higher and higher;
My fingers were white from holding on so tight.
Tears streamed down my cheeks,
Not through fear or fright, but from the wind.
I was amongst the clouds.
Another world appeared before me;
Everything below in my giant world became smaller.
I went higher and higher.
My brother's strong arms pushed harder.
I went faster backwards and forwards,
Like a pendulum on a clock.
Please, please, don't stop!

Piers Garland (12)
St James Independent School for Senior Boys, Twickenham

Hunger

Through the darkness, a lone howl.
A dark rogue against the moonlight.
It sniffs the cold, damp of the night.
Yellow eyes shine out through the sorrow

Far greater than my stale stare.
Ears emerge,
Then fangs.
A deep hunger

Searching through the darkness.
A lost soul,
An old friend long forgotten.
A noise, the window . . .

Hungrily, I turn towards it.
Then, a nose emerges,
Followed by a yellow stare.
A wolf, never having whet its appetite.

Sebastian Lawrence (12)
St James Independent School for Senior Boys, Twickenham

The Painting Of Life

In the first part of this painting
everything is beautiful,
wonderful birds sit in the trees.
In the second part,
it is still beautiful,
but a man points a gun at the birds.
In the third part,
it is dark and stormy,
all the birds are gone.
In the fourth part,
the storm has passed,
but the land is barren.
The fifth part is blank,
the artist lies dead on the floor.

Thomas Johnson (13)
St James Independent School for Senior Boys, Twickenham

The View Of The Harbour

The sun shone on boats creating a mysterious shadow
on the sea's surface.
Death was at the port serving fishes by the dozen.
Honour and pride were also there inviting young men to join them
jumping into the sea.
Humility was there for those who were not daring enough.
Lust was there welcoming all the young drooling men
that were staring at the ladies.
Envy was aboard the little boats envying the yachts and cruise liners.
Wrath was in the hearts of the lobsters who were snapping away
for their lives.
Greed was in the stomachs of all of the big boisterous beefy men
that were cramming plates of food into their mouths.
Disgust was in the heads of the men's wives and daughters.

Jaidev Singh Vohra (13)
St James Independent School for Senior Boys, Twickenham

The Mind Elephant

T rampling trees and making black prints in the snow with
H is large
E lephant feet.

M y room is light but
I n the darkness comes the elephant
N earer and nearer the darkness comes from the
D reary forest floor, the giant

E lephant lamely
L olls along still making prints in
E arly morning snow
P rinting the page. The snow is melting
H urrying from the half light the elephant gets to the edge
A nd the last line of the forest. The elephant goes on still
N ever to turn back. Going
T owards its goal in the sunrise.

Luke Weir (12)
St James Independent School for Senior Boys, Twickenham

The Thinka-Bug

I stare at the dew on the morning leaf:
Something else is there
Only the buzz of a bee for company
And this blank.

As I look, the sky is sunless:
Something nearer
Moving slowly through the stickiness
Towards the forgotten place.

Swiftly and silently, as the new leaf awakes,
The wings fold into the shell,
Six legs serve a movement, that scuttle and scuttle, and scuttle, and scuttle

Moves delicately over the leaf
Between stalks and stems
Antennae are sensing, picking up all movement
Of a body rich in colour.

Across a stump and over a branch, a bug
A twisting, winding pattern
Dazzling, glittering
Having its own way.

Till with a sudden jutter
It hits the floor
The sky is sunless still, the bee buzzes
The blank has ceased.

Jamie Parker (11)
St James Independent School for Senior Boys, Twickenham

Life

One day it will all start,
Your young eyes will open,
Your little eyelids will stretch,
And the first bit of light you see,
Pours in and fills the world.

You are only small and weak,
You go only a short way,
From the place you know so well,
Things will happen that make you proud,
But then you go and lose them.

One day you decide you've had enough,
And you will explore further,
And from places you never knew, you will find new things,
And you keep on going and growing,
Till you can stand up to things.

But it does not stop there,
You will keep on going, on and on,
You will gain vital knowledge,
And then once you share it out,
You will just fade and fall.

Dominic Purcell-Davis (13)
St James Independent School for Senior Boys, Twickenham

Writing A River

As I write, my pen reminds me of an otter,
gracefully swimming through rushing water.
The ink, the water, the nib the otter.
An otter is sleek and shiny, just like the silver of the nib.
The rush of the blue ink makes me think of a winding river
where the otter lives.
As the otter plays and gambols in the water, my poem grows.
Like the otter I need to reach the end,
me of my river of words, him, his resting place.
Sometimes the words come easily, like the otter at play.
Sometimes it's hard to write down my thoughts,
like an otter stalking a fish.

Joshua Daly (12)
St James Independent School for Senior Boys, Twickenham

Trail Of Mass Destruction

The pen is a shark,
Gliding through the sea.
The silent killer,
As silent as can be.

Twisting, turning, telling my mind,
Twisting, turning, the dead fish left behind.

The paper is the sea,
Teeming with life.
But all is hiding,
From the murderer with no knife.

Twisting, turning, telling my mind,
Twisting, turning, the dead fish left behind.

And the meal eaten,
The trail left,
The masterpiece done,
And that is that!

Will Dodsworth-Evans (12)
St James Independent School for Senior Boys, Twickenham

Bedtime Story

Underneath it all, under pretences,
Delusions and opinions doubt what I believe,
And what do my eyes see?
In all silence there is you and me.
So, if thoughts could be announced,
And truth is at ease,
Then would I know what you think?
Of all those around us and me.
Instead of questions and empty sentences,
And humour and chance,
Then and there alone, I would know,
What our smiles and glances show.
But blasted confusion, plagues everything!
And doubt's voice is never far remote.
And yet, if this is not meant to be,
And I am wasting youth and time,
Therefore, leave me with these illusions of 'nothing',
For they are too precious to desert,
Then I will keep this as a bedtime story,
And dream away about you with me.

Bambo Iyanu (John) Idowu-Agida (14)
St James Independent School for Senior Boys, Twickenham

The Desert Snake

In my study I sit,
The pen in my hand suddenly
And amazingly slips from my hand
And transforms into a hissing serpent.

As I move my hand
The paper turns into a desert,
And the snake begins to slither across the page,
Revealing words in the patterns of sand and stone as it moves.

It wriggles and writhes,
As I reach out to grab it,
it strikes!
Blue blood runs down my shirt.

The serpent prepares to strike again,
I see it has a downfall in its straight aim,
If you hold a tissue or any type of cloth up in front of it . . .
It will aim for that instead of your face.

This will leave time for you to study the snakes amazing twists
and twirls,
It never stops moving,
Always following one path,
And yet strangely.

Still has no idea of where it might be going,
It could be towards a dome,
Or a small grassy area where prey looms in every corner,
Suddenly it quickens its pace.

It spots something quite close,
It moves faster,
Faster,
Faster.

It catches its prey that is now in this pattern,
It leaves a small dot,
Showing where it has caught its prey,
Began a new journey and skipped an area again.

I stop grabbing,
It wriggles no more,
It has slunk through a small hole,
A small hole in the sand that is just visible.

The sand becomes page,
The sandstorm becomes rain,
It . . .
Is done.

Patrick Collins (12)
St James Independent School for Senior Boys, Twickenham

The Elusive Bulldog

Where could this bulldog be?
He's out there somewhere
Walking on the page:
Listening to the humming of the fridge
And the drip of the tap.

I hear no scratching at the door
Or no panting to let him in, nothing
He is out there somewhere waiting
Just for me!
Maybe not born yet.

So I sit thinking and waiting, begging
For him to come
Dirty paws on the kitchen floor
Appeals to me more and more
Everything is done.

Theodore Bucksey (12)
St James Independent School for Senior Boys, Twickenham

Space

Stars are whizzing past the wide panoramic screen,
Comets shuttle by leaving a trail on the eye,
Spaceships zoom by as if they had something to be done,
And urgently.
In a galaxy far, far away . . .
The most famous phrase in our dimension,
Yet what does it mean?
Our scientists contemplate the meaning of life,
Are there other life forms out there,
Or are we totally and utterly alone?
Space, the final frontier.

Louis Jent (13)
St James Independent School for Senior Boys, Twickenham

The Thought Of A Desert Animal

I imagine this midday moment's desert:
Something else wasn't still,
Something that moved every tick
Of my clock that said a minute.

Through the winter I see no birds,
But something a bit further away,
Something with a tail,
The colour of sand and bricks.

Hot, delicate as the bright sand,
The animal's ears perked up listening.
His head and ears going opposite directions,
And that moment was one again and again.

Set neat prints into the sand
Between cacti and near burrows,
But those prints despaired of the wind
So the page was never printed.

Adam Hodgson (12)
St James Independent School for Senior Boys, Twickenham

The Lion Kingdom

There the boy was writing about a lion,
Each word forming a brand new story,
Now into my imagination,
Into the heart of the lion,
Looking for his very wife.

The lion was shouting,
He was looking for his wife,
Until the middle of the forest gave him no mercy,
And the elephant was shown,
Behind that was this wife of his.

He fought and fought until he could do no more,
He was dead; his world had come to an end,
There was no more of the lion,
There he was, finished,
Each word forming a brand new story.

Harvinder Gill (12)
St James Independent School for Senior Boys, Twickenham

Alone

The wall stands there, the only
Thing that stops me is the wall
I hear their laughter, their fun
They're in for free
I pay and go to find them
They're gone
You wouldn't think it in a fair
But no one's there
I hate it; so many faces
All gorging themselves
But you see they see me
With disgust they think I'm no one
I am alone by myself; so many faces
But not one I know; not one of them
I am alone.

Joshua Parkinson (14)
St James Independent School for Senior Boys, Twickenham

The Bat's Life Journey

The bat has no fear,
Even though this is his first flight,
He flies with his elegant wings,
Spread out and skimming the cave.
But he bumps, crashes,
He is blind,
He feels dumb and good at nothing,
And it stops,
Now it has fear,
Where is he?
It screeches as if calling for help,
But nothing answers from the dark, dark cave.
What are those sounds he hears?
Click, click, click.
He doesn't care what it is because he knows where he is.
He gets back to his tunnel and rests for his next flight.
Then he thinks
He is not that useless,
He made his way back,
He found his sonar,
He stands up and flies away.
I hope like that bat, one day we all find our sonar.

Felix Burton (11)
St James Independent School for Senior Boys, Twickenham

The Dragon Of Hunting

The night sky is as dark as evil,
The cuckoo clock is tickless,
Thoughts not coming to me,
In the depth of darkness' red eyes.

Moving swiftly in the skies,
Red eyes quicker than the eyes,
Moving through the snow,

And trees,
Burning all it sees,
Leaving black printed trees.

Night still dark as evil,
Cuckoo clock still tickless,
Thoughts out of me,
No red eyes.

But the page is printed.

Shil Patel (11)
St James Independent School for Senior Boys, Twickenham

The Cat, Thought

I sit in my study,
The clock ticking loudly,
In the thought of a cat,
Standing very, very near.

Looking out wearily,
At all there is to see,
Minding its own business,
With not a care in the world.

As a car comes past,
It darts around wildly,
But is fast to regain its confidence.

Walking from car to car,
From driveway to driveway,
With still not a care in the world,
Just lying waiting to be stroked.

Then reality comes back,
There is no cat, no cars,
Not even any driveways,
But the emptiness of the room.

George Ford (12)
St James Independent School for Senior Boys, Twickenham

The Urban Cats

Gazing through the window, wondering.
The urban life:
People walk the streets day and night,
But there is more that lurks these streets,
Hiding beneath our noses, in the dustbins, in our homes,
On our rooftops.
Crawling on their toes, they live amongst us but not to all,
Some are cute,
Some are feared,
They all have a unique purr,
Those menacing eyes glow in the dark,
Watching your every move they leap,
Jump, hiss and scratch as your eyes follow theirs.
The roads are empty,
The poem is written,
The empty dark hole is filled,
With the tale of the urban cats!

Junaed Khan (12)
St James Independent School for Senior Boys, Twickenham

Lion

It was lying in the savannah
The wind blowing its fur
Under a tree it lay
Making a silent purr

His mane was a golden yellow
His paws have a leathery effect
His nose is a subtle pink
He holds his head erect.

Paisley Thomas (12)
The Arts Educational School, London

Denied War

An undefined bang, beats brashly in the distance
A failing, frozen wind sweeps the face of the mongers
A white drop of purity hits a metallic gold
And a roar is heard

A charging force of unbridled fury clears the field of any forgotten calm
And the wind is running in the ears of the fighters
And the white is stained by a fallen pool of burgundy
That beings to melt

The pain of one thousand screams hits the surrounding mountains
And the blood trickles into the furious and free river
A dark cloud of fire breath hits the sky
And so it is dark

A plain of bodies fills the air with disgust and dishonour
And the earth drinks the fertile blood of warriors
The smoking eyes of one army smothered by the will of another
And rain falls to wash it all away.

Oliver Horsfall (15)
The Arts Educational School, London

Viper

His poisonous kiss
His chilling hiss,
His deathly squeezing,
Can be alarmingly ceasing.

He slides and slithers
But never dithers,
When his prey is in sight,
A venomous bite,
Will be his victims,
Last goodnight.

Jamie Naylor (12)
The Arts Educational School, London

Guilty

Icy wind cutting through your heart,
The ring of the voices inside my ears,
Eyes glaring and staring upon my sides,
The rain pats me on the shoulder,
The trees whispering my name,
And my footprints glued to the floor.

My heart beating the blood around my body,
The word guilty stirring in my mind,
The moment replaying like a film,
But no one can know this crime,
Why did I do it you ask me?
Guilty, the word stares at me.

Who was it? Why was it?
Too many questions,
Are you guilty? When did it happen?
Stop asking!
Who? Where? Why? What?
Just stop, don't ask, I can't tell you.

The silence is piercing a hole in my body,
The hammer is falling again,
'Objection your honour!' he shouts,
He's guilty, he's guilty, or is he?
Are you? Tell the truth, but I can't
Stop! I'm guilty, I killed him.

Henrietta Hitchcock (13)
The Arts Educational School, London

Holocaust

Many years have long been gone,
though painful memories linger on.
Beneath a layer of ice-cold fear,
terrifying images reappear.
A churning train, a drumming beat,
the sickening smell of summer heat.
Two towering gates come into sight,
curious relief turns into fright.
Families cling to one another,
a crying child snatched from its mother.
A fearsome soldier shouts out a name,
a trembling man delirious with shame,
is grabbed by guards and thrown to the floor,
where his frail body trembles no more.

Jocie Juritz (13)
The Arts Educational School, London

Winter Wonderland

I stood beside a hill
Smooth with newly-laid snow
A single star looked out
From a cold evening glow.

There was no other creature
That saw what I could see
I stood and watched the evening star
As long as it watched me.

Angela Chen-Xie (12)
The Arts Educational School, London

The Beast Of Hell

It stays festering in Hell
Tied to one small post
Imbued with purpose fell
It lies in wait

For a person to let it free
So it can spread its wrath
And steal the only key
To the gate of paradise

Its wings fiery to the last
Its body scaly
And with one blast
Of its red-hot breath

It could melt the world
From the ice caps of Antarctica
To the curled
Boot of Italy

Its cat-like pose
Its feline eyes
With a quivering nose
On its two large heads

It waits, it waits
It will never die
Not when there is greed and malice in the world
It waits to be set free.

Katherine Paines (12)
The Godolphin & Latymer School, Hammersmith

Cat

Sleeping in the sun,
Tail curled protectively
Around the perfect body,
Kohl-rimmed eyes open slowly
As the afternoon siesta draws to a close.

Those eyes . . .
Like an amber traffic light
Or a roaring fire, lighting the world.
Eyes that have seen many things
Which no man has ever seen.

She moves silently,
Padding across the cool terracotta tiles
Of the kitchen.
She laps at a saucer of warm milk
With her sandpaper tongue.

A clumsy foot steps on her kinked tail,
How dare it?
Cat hisses like a goose,
Ears flattened on the domed head,
Her face reminds you of an angry brown owl.

Where does she come from,
This mystery cat?
Surely she is pure-bred
An Egyptian descendant,
This elegant cat.

But no,
This is a cat who was found
In a cardboard box,
In the pouring rain,
On Christmas Eve.

Anna Crossman (12)
The Godolphin & Latymer School, Hammersmith

A Smile

A smile warms me up on a frosty winter's morn,
A smile brightens me up on a dreary dawn.

A smile makes me happy on a sad day,
A smile makes me special when things haven't gone my way.

A smile calms me down when I am mad,
A smile shows compassion when I'm feeling bad.

A smile makes me friends I wished that I'd made,
A smile is a present that can't be weighed.

A smile is priceless but should be repaid.

Sara Langmuir (13)
The Godolphin & Latymer School, Hammersmith

The Daunting Docks

(A poem inspired by Arthur Grimshaw's painting of Liverpool Docks by moonlight)

The cracked street lamps reflect the muck on the empty street,
A horse-drawn cart passes by with great wheels like peat,
No longer do children's voices sing throughout the docks,
Instead, an empty silence and a creak from rusty locks.
The polluted buildings and worn-out masts tower over the dingy docks,
The small green shops are free of people scared off by wooden stocks,
The peeling posters on the old, white walls,
Dilapidated and ancient like the desolate market stalls.
The rotting wood has a foul musty smell,
As do the rats who scamper round the bell.
The ghost-like street has an eerie air,
A malevolent grin and a menacing stare.

Atalanta Fitzgerald (13)
The Godolphin & Latymer School, Hammersmith

If You . . .

If you could be black, white, Latin, Asian - any race you wanna be,
I'd love you.
If you respected yourself as you do others, I'd love you.
If you did things for the better of the world, I'd love you.
If you struggled to bring up a child at 15 years old and succeeded
I'd love you.
If you could change the bad name for kids today, I'd love you.
If the things that really mattered were presented in newspapers,
I'd love you.
If a member of my family didn't die and you managed to love them
more and more each day, I'd love you.
If you managed to love a stranger like your own son, I'd love you,
But for all this to happen, we need love for one another.

Joshua Buckmire (13)
The Waldorf School, London

Untitled

Your heart is pumping blood so fast
like you have run a race and come last
butterflies are in your chest
wiggly worms are in your hands
you can't sit down
you can't stand up
Run? Walk? Hop? Jump?
What to do? Where to go?
Your heart is pumping blood so fast
like you have run a race and come last.

Page Myrie-Audley (13)
The Waldorf School, London

Our School

I was sitting comfortably on my chair,
Watching 'Daredevil' without a care.
The phone rang, my mum picked it up,
'What? The school burnt down!' She hung up.

'Turn that off, we're going to check it out.'
'What right now?'
'Yes!'
'Do I have to?' I shout.
We ran to the bus to see it with our own eyes,
Down the path then we stopped in surprise.

Some ashy huts were all that remained,
I closed my eyes then looked again,
The wall had turned to dust,
The metal to rust,
And that was the end of the school.

Sam Eedle (13)
The Waldorf School, London

I Sit There Staring Up

I sit here on a grassy green
The sun hits my face like an abundance of warmth
The winds whisper to me as if to tell me secrets
I hear the faint sound of the city but intrude I will leave it not.

Here I am peaceful, I am a free soul
This shaded green beneath an old wise willow is my haven
Here in my haven, I am not judged
Not left to perish but given freedom.

This freedom is my wish
A universe full of expectation cannot exceed the calming nature
In which I find my cosy haven
Wished I.

Tesa De Haven (13)
The Waldorf School, London

Things That Used To Happen

Too many days passed without me seeing shapes
The faces go past, I don't know why
Too many people that I used to know
Like myself.

Too many lives gone down the drain
Just blank
I wanna live forever
Too bad
What's happening?
Who's that?
Wow!
Over there.

Yes, that's it
The dilapidated shack of the crippled wanderer
Why wander when you're crippled?
Because you're all perfect.

Limited imitation is a habit
No imagination to roam the floor
Why?
Too many questions, I'm going to bed.

Fearghall Kilkenny-Fletcher (13)
The Waldorf School, London